# ENKI AND THE WORLD ORDER

SCOTT MCCRARY

Copyright © 2024 by Scott McCrary

All rights reserved.

No part of this book may be reproduced in any form or by any electronic or mechanical means, including information storage and retrieval systems, without written permission from the author, except for the use of brief quotations in a book review.

*To Jennifer,*

*For being the calm in every storm, the wellspring of inspiration in every desert, and the harbor that always guides me home. This journey, like every great adventure we've embarked upon, is richer and more meaningful because you are by my side.*

Water is the driving force of all nature.

— LEONARDO DA VINCI

## CONTENTS

*Preface*   xi
*Introduction*   xvii

1. THE BIRTH OF ENKI   1
   Cosmic Origins   1
   Family Ties: Anunnaki Relations   2
   Enki's Creation: The Formation of Eridu   3
   The Assembly of the Gods   4
   Mythological Themes and Motifs   5
   Enki's Attributes and Symbols   5
   Early Worship and Cult Centers   6

2. ENKI AND THE COSMIC ORDER   8
   The Sumerian Creation Myth   8
   Enki's Role in Creation   9
   The Organization of the Universe   10
   Maintaining Cosmic Balance   10
   Enki's Wisdom and Knowledge   11
   Interactions with Humanity   12
   Myths of Order and Chaos   13

3. THE ME: DIVINE DECREES OF CIVILIZATION   14
   Understanding the Me   14
   Enki and the Transfer of Knowledge   15
   Civilization's Building Blocks   16
   The Me in Sumerian Society   17
   Mythical Narratives Involving the Me   18
   Enki's Benevolence and Trickery   19
   Impact on Mesopotamian Culture   20

4. ENKI, THE ENGINEER: MASTER OF WATERS AND CRAFTS   22
   The Abzu: Enki's Watery Domain   22
   Engineering and Architecture   23

Agriculture and Fertility 25
Crafts and Creations 26
Myths of Invention and Innovation 27
Enki as Patron of Artisans 28
Water as a Symbol of Life and Knowledge 29

5. ENKI AND THE GODS: RELATIONSHIPS
   AND RIVALRIES 30
   Enki and An: Father and Son Dynamics 30
   Enki and Ninhursag: Creativity and Conflict 31
   Enki and Inanna: The Transfer of the Me 32
   Enki and the Underworld 33
   Diplomacy and Deception 34
   Sibling Rivalry: Enki and Enlil 35
   Patron of Humanity vs. Divine Authority 35

6. ENKI'S OFFSPRING: THE PANTHEON
   EXPANDS 37
   Marduk: Rise of a God 37
   Ningizzida: Guardian of the Gate 38
   Dumuzid: The Shepherd King 39
   Nanshe: Goddess of Social Justice 40
   Divine Dynasties and Legacies 41
   The Role of Offspring in Enki's World Order 42
   Mythological Significance of Enki's Children 43

7. ENKI AND HUMANITY: CREATOR, SAVIOR,
   AND TRICKSTER 45
   The Creation of Humankind 45
   The Flood Myth: Enki's Warning 46
   Enki's Gifts to Humanity 47
   The Trickster God: Myths and Legends 48
   Enki's Role as Mediator 48
   Wisdom, Magic, and the Occult 49
   The Enduring Bond Between Enki and
   Humans 50

8. SACRED SITES AND CULT CENTERS 52
   Eridu: The First City 52
   The E-Abzu Temple 53
   Sacred Geography: Nippur and Uruk 54

|  |  |
|---|---|
| Pilgrimage and Worship Practices | 55 |
| Archaeological Discoveries | 56 |
| The Spread of Enki's Cult | 57 |
| Legacy of Sacred Sites | 58 |

9. **ENKI'S ADVERSARIES AND ALLIES** — 59
   - The Anunnaki Assembly — 59
   - Enki vs. Enlil: Order and Chaos — 60
   - Alliances with Goddesses — 61
   - Demons and Protective Spirits — 62
   - Cosmic Battles and Balance — 63
   - Enki's Diplomacy and Influence — 64
   - The Role of Adversaries in Mythology — 65

10. **RITUALS AND FESTIVALS** — 67
    - Annual Celebrations in Honor of Enki — 67
    - Rites of Passage and Initiation — 68
    - The Akitu Festival — 69
    - Water Rituals and Purification — 70
    - Magic and Incantations — 71
    - Priesthood and Temple Services — 72
    - The Legacy of Mesopotamian Rituals — 73

11. **SYMBOLS AND ICONOGRAPHY** — 75
    - The Goat-Fish and Capricorn — 75
    - The Caduceus and Modern Medicine — 76
    - Water as a Symbol of Life and Wisdom — 77
    - Enki's Throne and the Abzu — 78
    - Sacred Numbers and Geometry — 78
    - The Role of Artifacts in Worship — 79
    - Interpreting Ancient Art — 80

12. **ENKI IN LITERATURE** — 82
    - The Epic of Gilgamesh — 82
    - Enki and the World Order — 83
    - The Descent of Inanna — 84
    - Lamentations and Prayers — 85
    - Wisdom Literature and Proverbs — 86
    - Enki's Influence on Later Texts — 87
    - Comparative Analysis of Mythological Themes — 88

13. **COMPARATIVE MYTHOLOGY** — 90
    Enki and Egyptian Gods — 90
    Similarities with Greek Mythology — 91
    Parallels in Hindu and Buddhist Traditions — 92
    The Archetype of the Trickster — 93
    Water Deities Across Cultures — 94
    Enki and the Global Flood Myths — 95
    Syncretism and Cultural Exchange — 95

14. **ENKI'S LEGACY IN MODERN CULTURE** — 97
    Enki in New Age Beliefs — 97
    The God in Science Fiction and Fantasy — 98
    Enki in Popular Literature — 99
    Symbolism in Contemporary Art — 100
    Environmentalism and Enki — 101
    Digital Media and Video Games — 102
    The Relevance of Ancient Myths Today — 103

15. **THE FUTURE OF ENKI STUDIES** — 104
    Archaeological Prospects — 104
    Technological Advances in Research — 105
    Comparative Religion and Mythology — 106
    The Role of Digital Humanities — 107
    Reassessing Ancient Texts — 108
    Cultural and Spiritual Revival — 109
    Enki in the 21st Century and Beyond — 110

*Conclusion* — 113
*Glossary* — 119
*Suggested Readings* — 123

# PREFACE

## ACKNOWLEDGMENTS

Embarking on this journey to explore the depths of Enki's influence on the world order, I find myself deeply indebted to a constellation of individuals. The scholars, whose tireless work has illuminated the crumbled texts of ancient Mesopotamia, have been my north star. Equally, the conversations with contemporaries—those serendipitous exchanges that happen in the least expected moments—have injected this work with unforeseen insights and dimensions. It's these interactions, bridging the past and present, that have woven the rich tapestry this book aspires to be.

In the labyrinth of academia and beyond, mentors and peers alike have offered their wisdom, sometimes as structured advice, other times as offhand comments that struck a chord. Their contributions are the undercurrent that propels this narrative forward. To my family, for their patience and unwavering support, for understanding the long nights and the seemingly endless conversations with texts old enough to be myths themselves—thank you. This work, in many ways, is a testament to the collective spirit of inquiry that binds us all.

Lastly, the communities that have preserved these stories through centuries, whose cultural heritage forms the bedrock of our understanding of ancient civilizations, deserve our deepest respect and acknowledgment. Their oral histories, artifacts, and the landscapes that have shaped them and that they have shaped provide the context without which Enki's story would be untethered from the world it seeks to explain. This book is a tribute to their guardianship of history.

## WHY ENKI MATTERS

Enki occupies a space that is both enigmatic and profoundly relevant in the grand tapestry of ancient mythology. At first glance, his narratives offer a glimpse into the divine machinations of the ancient world, but a closer look reveals the timeless struggle between order and chaos, creativity and destruction, that defines the human condition. With his domain over water, knowledge, and life, Enki is not just a deity from ancient texts but a symbol of the forces that shape our world.

The stories of Enki resonate because they are stories of innovation, resilience, and the quest for balance. They speak to the heart of what it means to be human: to create, to destroy, and to restore. In our modern era, where the balance between nature and technology, tradition and innovation, is increasingly precarious, Enki's myths serve as a reminder of the need for wisdom and foresight. This book seeks to

# PREFACE

bridge the millennia, drawing lessons from Enki's world that are pertinent to our own challenges and aspirations.

Why Enki matters goes beyond academic interest or historical curiosity. It is about understanding the roots of human civilization and the enduring principles that have guided it through storms of change. We can examine our own society's attempts to navigate the complexities of the modern world through the lens of Enki's legacy, which is defined by his efforts to maintain harmony in the cosmos. This exploration is an invitation to reflect on our place within a continuum of human endeavor stretching back to the dawn of recorded history.

## METHODOLOGY

The methodology underpinning this exploration of Enki and the World Order is a tapestry of interdisciplinary research, narrative analysis, and speculative inquiry. Drawing upon the rich corpus of Mesopotamian literature, archaeological findings, and contemporary scholarship, this book endeavors to piece together the multifaceted persona of Enki and the cosmology he inhabits. By weaving together these diverse strands of evidence, the aim is to present a coherent narrative that respects the complexity of ancient beliefs while making them accessible to a modern audience.

This approach is not without its challenges. The ancient texts that serve as our primary sources are often incomplete and open to interpretation. To navigate this terrain, I have employed a comparative methodology, juxtaposing Mesopotamian myths with those of neighboring cultures to shed light on common themes and divergent motifs. This cross-cultural perspective not only enriches our under-

## PREFACE

standing of Enki but also situates his story within a broader narrative of human mythology and religious thought.

In engaging with these ancient texts, I have also been mindful of the historiographical debates that shape our understanding of the past. Where scholars diverge, I have sought to present a balanced view, highlighting the diversity of interpretations while offering my own insights. This book, therefore, is as much an invitation to dialogue as it is a presentation of facts. I hope that by exploring the many layers of Enki's story, readers will be inspired to consider the enduring questions of human existence that these ancient myths provoke.

### NAVIGATING THE TEXT

As we embark on this journey through the ancient world of Enki and the myriad forces that shaped the Mesopotamian worldview, it's important to consider how we navigate the complex narrative landscapes that await us. This book is structured to guide the reader through the intricate web of myths, legends, and historical insights that together illuminate the figure of Enki and his role in the world order. Each chapter is designed as a stepping stone, gradually building a comprehensive picture of Enki's multifaceted character and his impact on ancient society and beyond.

To make this journey as enriching as possible, I've interspersed the text with thematic explorations that delve deeper into specific aspects of Enki's domain, such as water, wisdom, and the art of creation and restoration. These thematic sections are intended to provide a richer understanding of the cultural and environmental contexts that shaped Mesopotamian mythology and, by extension, the

# PREFACE

narratives surrounding Enki. By approaching the text in this manner, readers are invited to explore the layers of meaning and symbolism that these ancient stories convey.

Furthermore, to aid in navigating the complexities of ancient Mesopotamian society and its pantheon, I've included cross-references to related myths, gods, and historical events. This interconnected approach not only highlights the interwoven nature of Mesopotamian religious and cultural life but also allows for a more dynamic exploration of the themes central to Enki's story. Whether you're a seasoned scholar of ancient history or a curious newcomer, this text aims to be a portal to a world where gods walked among men and where the forces of nature were the canvas for divine expression.

## A NOTE ON INTERPRETATION

In delving into the world of Enki and ancient Mesopotamia, we tread on ground that is both ancient and, in many ways, alien to our modern sensibilities. The interpretation of myths, especially those as rich and complex as those of Enki, is not a straightforward task. It requires a delicate balance between honoring the original context of these narratives and recognizing the lens through which we, as contemporary readers, view them. This book aims to navigate this balance with care, acknowledging the gaps in our understanding while striving to bring the essence of these ancient stories to life.

It's crucial to keep in mind that the myths of Enki, like all myths, underwent gradual evolution as a result of the shifting conditions in politics, society, and the environment. As a result, our interpretation of these tales is a dialogue with the past that incorporates the most recent archaeolog-

## PREFACE

ical findings, linguistic analyses, and theoretical insights from the disciplines of anthropology, psychology, and comparative religion. This book is an invitation to engage with these stories in a way that respects their origins and acknowledges their complexity.

Moreover, in interpreting these myths, we must also be aware of our own biases and the cultural assumptions that shape our understanding of the ancient world. By approaching Enki's stories with an open mind and a willingness to question, we can hope to uncover not just the beliefs and values of ancient Mesopotamia but also the universal themes that connect us to these distant ancestors. Through this exploration, Enki's world becomes a mirror in which we can reflect on our own relationship with the divine, the natural world, and the enduring human quest for knowledge and balance.

# INTRODUCTION

## THE WORLD OF MESOPOTAMIA

The Tigris and Euphrates rivers cradled Mesopotamia, where the symphony of human civilization first orchestrated its intricate melodies. This fertile crescent birthed cities that rose like dawn, each a testament to the ingenuity and spirit of its people. Here, the foundations of writing, agriculture, and law were laid, constructing the pillars of society we navigate today.

In this ancient tapestry, religion and culture were inseparably woven, with gods overseeing every aspect of human life and natural phenomena. The Mesopotamians lived their lives under a celestial dome of divine watchfulness, where deities dictated the fate of humanity and the universe. Their beliefs were mirrored in ziggurats that scraped the skies and prayers that whispered through the winds, a constant dialogue between the mortal and the divine.

INTRODUCTION

Amidst this divine pantheon stood figures of profound influence, deities who shaped the contours of Mesopotamian faith and culture. Among them, Enki, the god of water, wisdom, and creation, commanded a unique reverence. His narratives, etched in clay, reveal the depth of his wisdom and the breadth of his domain, marking him as a central figure in understanding this ancient world.

## WHO WAS ENKI?

Enki, known as the master shaper of the world, held dominion over the abzu, the deep waters that nourish the earth. He was a deity of contradictions: a creator and protector, a trickster, and a teacher. Enki's essence was that of life-giving water flowing into the fields of human existence, yet his currents often carried the seeds of chaos and change.

His stories are myriad, each a facet of his complex personality. Enki's role in the creation of humanity, his rebellion against divine orders for the sake of his creations, and his cunning intellect that both solved and stirred troubles paint a picture of a god whose love for humanity was as deep as the waters he ruled. Through Enki, the Mesopotamians explored themes of creativity, wisdom, and the ambivalent nature of existence.

Yet, it was Enki's profound wisdom and his guardianship over the me, the divine laws, that established him as a pivotal figure in Mesopotamian mythology. He navigated the divine and mortal realms with ease, a mediator and an instigator whose actions often reflected the complex relationship between gods and humans. Enki's tales, rich with symbolism, offer invaluable insights into the ancient Mesopotamian worldview.

INTRODUCTION

## THE CONCEPT OF WORLD ORDER

The Mesopotamian concept of world order, or me, was an intricate framework that governed the cosmos, society, and the individual. It was the divine order that brought harmony to chaos, a set of laws and decrees that all beings, gods and humans alike, were bound to. Enki, as the keeper of the me, played a crucial role in maintaining this cosmic balance; his wisdom was often the key to resolving the celestial and terrestrial upheavals.

This divine order was not static; it reflected the dynamic and often tumultuous relationship between the deities and their creations. Enki, with his deep understanding of the me, was able to navigate these waters, sometimes bending the rules to protect what he held dear. His actions, driven by a profound empathy for mankind, often put him at odds with other gods, highlighting the tension between predestined order and the chaotic nature of life.

Enki's interventions shed light on the Mesopotamian belief that a balance of forces governs the universe. It was a balance that required vigilance and wisdom to maintain, qualities that Enki exemplified. His role in these cosmic dramas underscores the importance of knowledge, creativity, and cunning in navigating the currents of fate, themes that resonate with the human condition across ages.

## MYTHS AND LEGENDS SURROUNDING ENKI

The myths and legends that swirl around Enki are as diverse as the waters he governs. From the creation of humanity from clay to the epic quest to retrieve the sacred laws, the me, from the abyss, each story serves as a testament to his

INTRODUCTION

wit, his compassion, and his indefatigable spirit. These tales not only entertained but served a deeper purpose, embedding in the collective consciousness the values, fears, and aspirations of the Mesopotamian people.

In one famed narrative, Enki challenges the decree of the divine assembly to save humanity from the deluge, a story that echoes through the ages and finds its parallels in flood myths around the world. Enki's defiance of his peers' predetermined fate emphasizes his position as mankind's guardian and demonstrates his willingness to challenge even the highest authorities for the benefit of his creations. It's a theme that resonates deeply, reflecting the complex relationship between creator and creation.

Yet, another legend recounts Enki's descent into the underworld, a journey that illuminates the depths of his character and the breadth of his domain. These stories, rich with metaphor and meaning, offer a window into the ancient soul, revealing a worldview where gods and humans interact in a shared landscape of dreams and reality. Enki, with his dual nature, embodies the essence of this interplay, bridging the chasm between the divine and the mortal with his deeds and his wisdom.

SYMBOLS AND ICONOGRAPHY

The symbols and iconography associated with Enki are as layered and profound as the deity himself. Often depicted with the streams of water that are his domain, Enki's imagery is imbued with the life-giving essence of the liquid element. These symbols not only represent his power over the waters but also signify his role as the nurturer of civilization, the bringer of fertility and wisdom to the land and its people.

The goat-fish, a creature that encapsulates the amalgamation of terrestrial and aquatic life, stands as a prominent symbol of Enki's dual nature. It represents his mastery over both realms—a deity who easily traverses the boundaries of the world. This iconography, steeped in the lore of ancient astrology, later evolved into the constellation Capricorn, carrying with it the legacy of Enki across time and cultures.

Equally symbolic is the Euphrates itself, which, according to legend, flowed from Enki's shoulders, further cementing his connection to the lifeblood of Mesopotamia. These symbols, rich in meaning, weave a visual narrative of Enki's influence, portraying him as a guardian of the cosmic order and a patron of humanity's quest for knowledge and survival.

## ENKI'S INFLUENCE BEYOND SUMER

Enki's influence, much like the waters he commands, flowed far beyond the borders of Sumer, seeping into the cultures and religions that followed. Following civilizations adopted and modified his traits and deeds, demonstrating the malleability of myth and the enduring nature of his persona. As Ea, he continued to be revered in Akkadian and Babylonian cultures, a testament to his lasting impact on the ancient Near East.

This cross-cultural journey of Enki/Ea highlights the universal themes that his myths encapsulate: creation, wisdom, and the fraught relationship between the divine and the human. These themes, transcending geographical and temporal boundaries, resonate with the fundamental questions of existence. They exhibit a common heritage of attempting to understand a world under the control of forces beyond human control.

The legacy of Enki in modern interpretations continues to evolve, with scholars, writers, and spiritual seekers finding in his stories a source of inspiration and insight. His character serves as a bridge connecting the ancient past with contemporary thought, inviting reflection on the nature of knowledge, power, and our place within the cosmos. Enki's enduring relevance speaks to the timeless quest for meaning that defines the human experience.

## MODERN INTERPRETATIONS OF ENKI

In the landscape of modern thought, Enki has emerged as a figure of intrigue and speculation, his ancient mythos offering rich fodder for contemporary interpretation. Scholars dissect his legends, seeking insights into the Mesopotamian worldview, while psychologists draw parallels between Enki's narratives and the archetypal journeys of the human psyche. This multifaceted deity, with his complex web of attributes, provides a mirror reflecting our own dilemmas and aspirations.

Among the spiritual and New Age communities, Enki is often seen as a symbol of esoteric wisdom and the pursuit of inner knowledge. His defiance against the divine order, his empathy towards humanity, and his mastery over the creative and destructive forces of water make him a potent symbol of transformation and enlightenment. In this modern context, Enki's story is revisited as a guide to personal growth and understanding of the natural world.

# INTRODUCTION

Moreover, Enki's mythos has found its way into popular culture, inspiring artworks, literature, and even discussions on environmental stewardship, highlighting his relevance in debates about humanity's relationship with the natural environment. As we navigate the complexities of the modern world, Enki's ancient wisdom serves as a reminder of the enduring power of myth to inspire, challenge, and transform.

# THE BIRTH OF ENKI

## COSMIC ORIGINS

Before the world as we know it took shape, there was a vast, swirling chaos—an endless expanse where the seeds of the cosmos lay dormant. Within this primordial soup, Enki emerged as a beacon of creation, his essence intertwined with the life-giving and unpredictable nature of water. This narrative of Enki's birth from the cosmic abyss speaks volumes about the Mesopotamian understanding of the universe's origins, portraying it as an intricate dance of elemental forces with water at its core. Enki's emergence from this chaos symbolized not just the birth of a deity but the genesis of order, knowledge, and life itself, setting the stage for the unfolding of the world and civilization.

The tale of Enki's cosmic beginnings mirrors the Mesopotamian people's reverence for the natural elements around them, especially water, as the fundamental building block of life. By attributing the origin of this crucial deity to the very essence of creation, they underscored the interconnectedness of the divine with the natural world. Enki, in his role as the god of water, becomes a symbol of both the nurturing and destructive aspects of nature, embodying the duality that is inherent in the world. This portrayal reflects the ancient Mesopotamians' deep understanding of their environment, acknowledging the power and unpredictability of the natural forces that shaped their lives.

## FAMILY TIES: ANUNNAKI RELATIONS

Enki's familial connections within the Anunnaki pantheon highlight his central role in cosmic and earthly affairs. Son of Anu, the sky god, and Nammu, the goddess of the ancient sea, Enki's lineage endowed him with a unique blend of celestial authority and the primordial power of creation. His siblings, including Enlil, the air god, and Inanna, the goddess of love and war, provided a complex web of relationships that influenced the dynamics of divine interaction. These ties were not merely symbolic; they represented the Mesopotamian belief in the fundamental interconnectedness of all aspects of life and the cosmos, with Enki serving as a pivotal figure bridging the realms of earth, sky, and water.

The intricate narratives surrounding Enki and his divine kin reflect the Mesopotamians' attempts to understand and explain the natural and social orders. Through the lens of these familial relationships, themes of conflict, cooperation, and balance are explored, mirroring the human experience. Enki, often depicted as a mediator among the gods, embodies the qualities of wisdom, diplomacy, and inventiveness. His role in resolving disputes and imparting knowledge to both gods and humans alike underscores the value placed on harmony, intelligence, and creativity in Mesopotamian society.

## ENKI'S CREATION: THE FORMATION OF ERIDU

Eridu's establishment as the first city by Enki is a testament to his powers of creation and civilization. This act of founding Eridu was more than a mere architectural endeavor; it was a symbolic gesture, marking the transition from chaos to order, from untamed nature to structured society. In Eridu, Enki's wisdom and generosity flourished as he bestowed upon humanity the gifts of agriculture, law, and writing. These contributions were fundamental to the development of civilization, reflecting the god's overarching role as a patron of human progress and a guardian of cosmic balance.

The formation of Eridu under Enki's guidance can be seen as the Mesopotamians' narrative attempt to grapple with the origins of their own society and the forces that shape the natural and social world. This story, rich with symbolic meaning, speaks to the ancient belief in the divine as the source of life's necessities and the arbiter of fate. Enki's establishment of Eridu, therefore, is not just a mythological account but a reflection of the deep-seated human desire to understand our beginnings and the elements that contribute to the sustenance and advancement of society.

Through these stories, Enki emerges not only as a god of water and wisdom but as a foundational figure in the Mesopotamian conception of the world. His birth from the cosmic abyss, his complex family ties, and his role in founding Eridu illustrate the interconnectedness of divine action, natural forces, and human civilization. Enki's narratives serve as a bridge between the heavens and the earth, offering insights into the ancient Mesopotamians' understanding of their place in the cosmos and their reverence for the forces that govern existence.

## THE ASSEMBLY OF THE GODS

Within the celestial hierarchy, the assembly of the gods represented the pinnacle of divine governance, a forum where the deities convened to deliberate on matters affecting both heaven and earth. Enki, with his unparalleled wisdom and foresight, played a crucial role in these gatherings, often acting as a mediator and advisor. His contributions were not merely suggestions but were pivotal in shaping the outcomes of divine debates, highlighting his significance beyond his immediate domain of water and wisdom. This assembly, much like a council of elders in Mesopotamian cities, mirrored the societal structures familiar to the people of the time, embodying the idea that even the gods must collaborate and negotiate to maintain harmony in the universe.

The dynamics within the assembly of the gods also served to explore themes of justice, authority, and the balance of power. Enki, often in opposition to his brother Enlil, brought a perspective that balanced assertiveness with compassion and innovation with tradition. While celestial in setting, these stories offered the people of Mesopotamia a reflection on their own governance and social order, encouraging a society where wisdom and understanding could avert conflict and foster prosperity. Through Enki's actions and interventions, the ancient texts advocate for a world where balance and foresight lead to stability and growth.

## MYTHOLOGICAL THEMES AND MOTIFS

Enki's myths are woven with a rich tapestry of themes and motifs that resonate with universal aspects of the human experience. Through tales of creation, trickery, and salvation, Enki embodies the dual nature of existence, where chaos and order, destruction and creation, are inextricably linked. These stories reflect not only the Mesopotamian understanding of the world but also their values and ethics, portraying Enki as a god who champions humanity, offering gifts of knowledge and protection. For example, the myth of Enki and the world order illustrates the importance of wisdom and cunning over brute force, proposing that understanding and intellect can prevail over adversity.

Moreover, Enki's narratives delve into the complexities of responsibility and the consequences of divine and mortal actions. His interactions with other gods, humans, and creatures highlight the interconnectedness of all beings and the ripple effects of decisions made within the cosmic hierarchy. Through these mythological explorations, the Mesopotamians engaged with ideas about fate, free will, and the moral obligations of power, embedding in their stories a sophisticated philosophical inquiry into the nature of life and the cosmos.

## ENKI'S ATTRIBUTES AND SYMBOLS

The attributes and symbols associated with Enki are as multifaceted as the deity himself, each emblematic of different aspects of his dominion and character. The streams and rivers, fundamental to Mesopotamian life and culture, signify Enki's control over the waters and his role as a life-giver and sustainer. The goat-fish, a chimera representing fertility and the dual nature of Enki's powers, encapsulates his connection to both the land and the sea. Furthermore, the E-abzu, Enki's temple in Eridu, stands as a symbol of his wisdom and the center of his worship, where the sacred waters flow and the mysteries of the universe are kept.

These symbols, deeply ingrained in Mesopotamian art and architecture, served as constant reminders of Enki's presence and influence. They were not merely decorative but were imbued with meaning, acting as conduits between the divine and the mortal realms. Through these icons, the ancient Mesopotamians expressed their understanding of the world and their place within it, encapsulating their fears, hopes, and reverence for the forces that shaped their existence. Enki's attributes and symbols, therefore, are more than mythological motifs; they are reflections of a culture's attempt to articulate the fundamental principles of life, nature, and the divine.

## EARLY WORSHIP AND CULT CENTERS

The worship of Enki centered around the temple of E-abzu in Eridu but extended throughout Mesopotamia, reflecting the deep reverence held for this deity. As the god of wisdom, water, and creation, Enki's cult attracted followers from all walks of life, from the highest priests to the humblest farmers, all seeking his blessings and guidance. The rituals and offerings performed in his honor were not mere acts of devotion but were seen as essential to maintaining the balance of the natural world and ensuring the prosperity of the community. These practices, rich in symbolism and steeped in tradition, underscored the reciprocal relationship between the divine and the mortal, a bond that was central to Mesopotamian religious belief.

The architecture and organization of Enki's cult centers, particularly in Eridu, were designed to reflect the cosmic order that Enki himself helped to establish. The layout of the E-abzu, with its intricate water systems mimicking the natural flow of rivers, served as a microcosm of the world, a sacred space where heaven and earth met. This design was not only an architectural feat but also a physical manifestation of Mesopotamian cosmology, embodying the interconnectedness of all things.

The legacy of Enki's worship, with its emphasis on wisdom, creation, and the harmonious balance between the forces of nature, continues to fascinate scholars and laypersons alike. Through the study of ancient texts, artifacts, and temple ruins, we gain insight into the profound impact that Enki and his cult had on Mesopotamian society. These early centers of worship were not just places of religious observance but were hubs of cultural and intellectual activity, where the mysteries of the cosmos were explored, and the foundations of civilization were strengthened. Enki's enduring influence on Mesopotamian culture underscores the lasting power of myth to shape human understanding and the way we relate to the world around us.

# ENKI AND THE COSMIC ORDER

## THE SUMERIAN CREATION MYTH

The Sumerian creation myth opens, not with a bang, but with the murmur of water, an endless, formless sea that predates consciousness itself. Into this void, Enki, the deity of wisdom and waters, introduces the first semblance of order. He separates the heavens from the earth, carves the rivers and seas, and sets the stage for the emergence of life. This myth, steeped in the awe of creation, reveals the Mesopotamians' reverence for the natural world and their belief in a universe born from divine intervention. Enki's role as a creator establishes him not just as a force of nature, but as the architect of the world's order, highlighting the intrinsic link between water and life in the Sumerian worldview.

In the narrative fabric of this myth, Enki emerges as a mediator between chaos and order, embodying the transformative power of water to both give life and destroy it. His actions are a testament to the dual nature of existence, where creation is inextricably linked to destruction and life to death. This duality is central to the Sumerian understanding of the cosmos, where balance is achieved not through the dominance of one force over another but through their harmonious coexistence. The Sumerians developed a sophisticated cosmology through Enki, one that views the universe as dynamic, ever-evolving, and shaped by the interaction of elemental forces.

## ENKI'S ROLE IN CREATION

Enki's contribution to the cosmos goes beyond the mere act of creation; he imbues the world with wisdom, laying down the foundations for civilization. As the god of water, he is inherently linked to the concepts of fertility and growth, but his domain extends to the intellectual and cultural realms, offering humanity the tools needed to thrive. Through his guidance, the earliest cities took shape along the banks of the rivers he sculpted, and the seeds of society were sown. Enki's role in this process underscores a profound respect for knowledge and learning in Sumerian culture, casting him as a patron of both the physical and intellectual aspects of civilization.

His interactions with the world and its inhabitants are characterized by a deep benevolence and a desire to see life flourish in all its forms. Enki, in his wisdom, recognizes the potential for greatness within humanity, and through his gifts of knowledge and craft, he empowers them to realize it. This relationship between deity and mortal is not one of subservience but of collaboration, with Enki acting as a mentor and guide. It's a dynamic that reflects the Sumerian belief in the interconnectedness of all things, where gods and humans, nature and culture, are part of a single, intricate web of existence.

## THE ORGANIZATION OF THE UNIVERSE

The Sumerians conceived the universe as a meticulously structured entity, with Enki playing a pivotal role in its organization. This structure mirrors the hierarchical society of Mesopotamia itself, with deities presiding over various aspects of the natural and divine worlds. Enki, with his domain over the waters that are the source of all life, occupies a central position in this cosmic order. His responsibilities extend beyond the creation of physical spaces to the establishment of the rhythms and cycles that govern the natural world, ensuring the continuity of life through the seasons.

This organization of the universe is not merely a reflection of the Sumerians' observations of the natural world but a manifestation of their deeper philosophical inquiries into the nature of existence. Enki's role in maintaining the balance between the forces of creation and destruction, order and chaos, speaks to a nuanced understanding of the universe as a complex, dynamic system. It's a system where harmony is achieved not through the suppression of opposing forces but through their integration and balance.

## MAINTAINING COSMIC BALANCE

In the grand cosmic scheme, Enki's role transcends the mere act of creation; he is the maintainer of balance, ensuring that the forces of order and chaos remain in equilibrium. This task requires not only power but profound wisdom, qualities that Enki possesses in abundance. His interventions, often subtle and always informed by a deep understanding of the natural order, prevent the universe from slipping back into primordial chaos. This aspect of Enki's deity highlights the Sumerian view that balance is not a given but something that must be actively maintained, a process that requires vigilance, wisdom, and a deep understanding of the interconnectedness of all things.

Enki's methods for maintaining cosmic balance are as varied as the challenges he faces. His philosophy favors peace over conquest and wisdom over force, which guides his actions in everything from mediating disputes between the gods to preventing natural disasters. These tales of Enki's interventions serve as allegories for the Sumerian people, teaching them the importance of balance in their own lives and societies. Through these stories, Enki becomes a model for leadership, embodying the ideals of foresight, compassion, and deep respect for the natural order.

## ENKI'S WISDOM AND KNOWLEDGE

The wisdom and knowledge of Enki are legendary, encompassing not only the secrets of the physical world but also the mysteries of the divine realm. His understanding of the universe is unparalleled, making him a revered figure among gods and humans alike. This reverence is not merely for his intellect but for his willingness to share his knowledge and to teach and guide those around him. Enki's wisdom is a beacon that illuminates the path to understanding, a gift that fosters growth, innovation, and harmony within the cosmos.

His teachings, passed down to humanity, laid the foundations for civilization, shaping the cultures, laws, and technologies that define Sumerian society. These lessons are not dictatorial edicts but invitations to explore, understand, and co-create with the divine. The openness and cooperation that characterize Enki's approach to knowledge highlight the Sumerian belief in the ability of education to change both individuals and societies. Through his example, the Sumerians are encouraged to seek wisdom, to question and explore the world around them, and to find their place within the cosmic order.

## INTERACTIONS WITH HUMANITY

Enki's interactions with humanity are marked by profound empathy and a genuine desire to uplift and protect. Unlike deities, who may view humans as mere subjects or playthings, Enki sees them as partners in the ongoing project of creation. He intervenes on their behalf, not just to save them from divine wrath or natural calamities but to empower them with knowledge and skills. These acts of benevolence are not born of obligation but of a deep-seated belief in humanity's potential to contribute to the cosmic order.

Through myths and legends, Enki's relationship with humans is depicted as one of mentorship and guidance. He teaches them agriculture, writing, and the arts, tools that enable them to build societies and express their understanding of the world. These stories, while mythical, reflect the Sumerians' appreciation for the divine as a source of inspiration and knowledge, a force that enriches their lives and pushes them toward greater achievements.

## MYTHS OF ORDER AND CHAOS

The myths surrounding Enki, particularly those dealing with the themes of order and chaos, are more than mere stories; they are profound reflections on the nature of existence. Enki, straddling the line between these two primal forces, embodies the complexity of the cosmos, a realm where order is constantly emerging from chaos and destruction paves the way for new creation. These narratives explore the delicate balance that sustains the universe, a balance that Enki, with his deep wisdom and power, is uniquely positioned to maintain.

These myths serve as allegories, teaching the Sumerians—and, by extension, us—about the importance of balance, resilience, and adaptability. Enki's ability to navigate the tumultuous waters of cosmic chaos to find harmony amidst discord offers valuable lessons on how to confront the challenges of life. His story encourages us to embrace the uncertainty of existence, to recognize the potential for growth and renewal in every challenge, and to see ourselves as active participants in the ongoing creation of the world.

In the figure of Enki, the Sumerians found not just a god to worship but a symbol of their deepest values and aspirations. Through the myths and stories that surround him, they explored the fundamental questions of their existence, finding in his wisdom a guide for living in harmony with the cosmos. Enki's legacy, as captured in these ancient texts, continues to inspire, reminding us of the enduring power of myth to shape our understanding of the world and our place within it.

# THE ME: DIVINE DECREES OF CIVILIZATION

## UNDERSTANDING THE ME

In the heart of Sumerian civilization lies a concept as foundational as the bricks that built the ziggurats: the Me. These are not just rules or laws but the very DNA of society, encompassing everything from moral codes to the techniques of agriculture, from the rituals of worship to the art of governance. The Me represents the divine order imposed on the chaos of the natural world, a sacred set of decrees that define the roles, behaviors, and structures of Sumerian society. Enki, as the keeper of the Me, holds a pivotal role in this cosmic framework, serving as the conduit through which these divine principles are disseminated among the gods and to humanity.

This transfer of the Me from the divine to the earthly realm is a testament to Enki's integral role in the formation and maintenance of civilization. His actions, steeped in wisdom and foresight, ensured that humanity was endowed with the

# ENKI AND THE WORLD ORDER

knowledge necessary to thrive. Enki's distribution of the Me was not arbitrary; it was a deliberate act meant to foster order, prosperity, and harmony within the human world. Through the Me, Enki laid the groundwork for societal development, embedding in humanity the seeds of progress and civilization.

The significance of the Me in Sumerian society cannot be overstated. These divine decrees were the blueprint upon which the entirety of Sumerian civilization was constructed. They informed not only the practical aspects of daily life but also the spiritual, linking the human experience directly to the divine. The Me ensured that every action, from the weaving of cloth to the construction of cities, was imbued with a deeper, sacred meaning. In this way, the Me served as a constant reminder of the divine order, guiding the Sumerians in their quest to live in harmony with the will of the gods.

## ENKI AND THE TRANSFER OF KNOWLEDGE

The transfer of the Me from Enki to humanity marks one of the most profound moments in Mesopotamian mythology. It symbolizes not just the passing of knowledge but the empowerment of mankind, the divine endorsement for humanity to build, create, and govern according to the principles of the gods. Enki's role in this transfer showcases his unique position as both a creator and a teacher, a god who not only shapes the physical world but also nurtures the intellectual and spiritual growth of its inhabitants.

This act of transmission is imbued with great ceremony and significance, reflecting the deep respect the Sumerians held for knowledge and its divine origins. Enki's benevolence in sharing the Me underscores a fundamental belief in the potential of humanity to mirror the divine and embody the order and complexity of the cosmos in their societies. Through this gift, Enki sets into motion the advance of civilization, a testament to his foresight and his commitment to the welfare of the human race.

The implications of this transfer reverberate through Sumerian culture, establishing a legacy of learning and innovation. The Me, as the foundation of all societal advancements, becomes a symbol of humanity's capacity for growth and development. Through Enki's wisdom, the Sumerians are encouraged to explore, build, and contemplate the mysteries of the universe, forever linking their cultural achievements to the divine will expressed through the Me.

## CIVILIZATION'S BUILDING BLOCKS

The Me functioned as the building blocks of Sumerian civilization, a comprehensive system of divine ordinances that dictated every aspect of societal life. These decrees cover a broad spectrum, from the arts and crafts essential for economic development to the rituals and ceremonies that underpin religious practice. In essence, the Me provides a template for living, a set of guidelines that ensure the smooth functioning of society and its alignment with divine order.

The integration of the Me into the fabric of Sumerian society illustrates the profound impact of these divine decrees on the development of early civilization. They are not merely rules to be followed but are considered gifts from the gods, imbued with sacred significance. This perspective fosters a culture of reverence and duty towards upholding the cosmic order, with the Me serving as a constant reminder of the divine presence in everyday life.

The influence of the Me extends beyond the practicalities of governance and ritual, shaping the very consciousness of the Sumerian people. They instill a sense of purpose and identity, linking individual actions to the broader narrative of cosmic harmony. Through the Me, the Sumerians understand their place in the universe, not as mere subjects of divine whim but as active participants in the maintenance of order. Enki, through his gift of the Me, empowers humanity with a sense of agency, embedding in the culture a legacy of cooperation between the divine and the mortal, which continues to inspire and inform long after the fall of Sumerian civilization.

## THE ME IN SUMERIAN SOCIETY

The Me's integration into Sumerian society was profound, touching every aspect of life and elevating daily practices to expressions of divine will. These decrees were seen not merely as instructions from the gods but as the very pillars upon which society stood. Each Me, from those governing the rites of the priesthood to those dictating the methods of agriculture, was infused with a sense of sacred duty, binding the community in a collective pursuit of harmony and order. This reverence for the Me underscored the Sumerians' belief in a world where human actions were deeply entwined with the divine, where each task, no matter how mundane, carried with it a cosmic significance.

In this light, the role of the priest-king, or lugal, was central to the administration of the Me within the city-states. Tasked with the earthly stewardship of these divine decrees, the lugal served as a bridge between the gods and the people, ensuring that society reflected the heavenly order. This responsibility underscored the theocratic nature of Sumerian governance, where political power was deeply interwoven with religious authority. The Me, therefore, were not just spiritual guidelines but a framework for societal organization, embodying the principles of justice, equity, and wisdom that were essential to the maintenance of social order.

The impact of the Me on Sumerian culture extended beyond the practicalities of law and governance, shaping the very identity of its people. Art, literature, and architecture were all influenced by these divine decrees, with temples, ziggurats, and public works serving as physical manifestations of the Me's principles. Through these cultural expressions, the Sumerians celebrated their relationship with the divine, crafting a civilization that was a testament to their understanding of the cosmos. The Me, as interpreted and implemented by figures like Enki, became the blueprint for a society that sought to mirror the harmony and complexity of the universe, a legacy that continues to inspire awe and wonder.

MYTHICAL NARRATIVES INVOLVING THE ME

The myths surrounding the Me are not mere stories but reflections of the Sumerians' deepest values and fears. In these narratives, the Me serves as both a prize and a burden, a symbol of divine favor and the weighty responsibility that comes with it. One of the most compelling tales involves Enki's decision to grant these decrees to humanity, a move that is fraught with tension and conflict among the gods.

# ENKI AND THE WORLD ORDER

This story, rich with themes of power, wisdom, and the quest for order, highlights the complex relationship between the divine and the mortal, underscoring the Sumerians' belief in the benevolence and guidance of gods like Enki.

Within these myths, Enki often emerges as a trickster figure, using his wits and wisdom to navigate the challenges posed by the Me's distribution. His actions, though sometimes deceptive, are ultimately aimed at securing the best outcomes for humanity, demonstrating a deep understanding of the delicate balance required to maintain cosmic harmony. These tales articulate the Sumerians' nuanced view of the divine, portraying gods who are not infallible but are deeply engaged in the ongoing project of creation and order. Through Enki's adventures, the Sumerians explore the tensions between chaos and order, freedom and destiny, imbuing their mythology with a rich tapestry of moral and existential dilemmas.

## ENKI'S BENEVOLENCE AND TRICKERY

Enki's distribution of the Me encapsulates his dual nature as both a benevolent protector and cunning trickster. His benevolence is evident in his eagerness to equip humanity with the means to build a just and prosperous society. However, the methods Enki employs often involve subterfuge and cleverness, revealing a complexity to his character that the Sumerians deeply admired. This duality reflects a broader theme in Sumerian mythology: that wisdom and knowledge are tools that, when wielded with skill and understanding, can navigate the murky waters of divine and mortal politics.

The trickery associated with Enki, particularly in the tales of the Me's transfer, is not malicious but serves a higher purpose. It highlights the importance of intellect and creativity in overcoming obstacles, suggesting that adherence to strict rules is less valuable than the ability to think innovatively. Through these stories, the Sumerians celebrated the power of cunning and strategy, elevating Enki as a model of adaptability and ingenuity. His actions remind us that the path to harmony often requires navigating complexity with a blend of knowledge, wit, and foresight.

## IMPACT ON MESOPOTAMIAN CULTURE

The Me's influence on Mesopotamian culture is immeasurable, permeating every facet of life and leaving a lasting legacy on the ancient world. Through the organization and dissemination of these divine decrees, Enki played a pivotal role in shaping the moral, social, and technological landscape of Sumerian civilization. The Me provided a framework for understanding the world, a set of principles that guided the Sumerians in their quest for harmony between the human and the divine. This interplay between the earthly and the celestial fostered a culture that valued wisdom, justice, and the pursuit of knowledge, principles that remain cornerstones of human civilization.

The enduring legacy of the Me and Enki's role in their stewardship reflects the profound impact of mythology on cultural identity and societal development. These stories passed down through generations, served not only as religious doctrine but as a moral compass, shaping the values and behaviors of the Sumerian people. In the figure of Enki and the narrative of the Me, we see the embodiment of the

Sumerians' deepest aspirations: to live in a world ordered by justice, enriched by knowledge, and guided by the divine. The Me's impact on Mesopotamian culture underscores the timeless human quest for order and meaning in a chaotic universe, a quest that continues to inspire and challenge us today.

# ENKI, THE ENGINEER: MASTER OF WATERS AND CRAFTS

## THE ABZU: ENKI'S WATERY DOMAIN

Enki, the Sumerian god of knowledge, water, and craft, is in charge of the Abzu, a realm teeming with the first waters of creation. This sacred place, from which all fresh waters are believed to flow, represents not only the physical source of life's sustenance but also the wellspring of Enki's boundless creativity. It is here, in the deep, that Enki's connection to the elemental force of water transcends mere dominion, embodying the profound relationship between the divine and the life-giving waters that sustain the world. The Abzu, with its mysterious depths, stands as a testament to the ancient Mesopotamians' reverence for water as a fundamental, life-affirming element in their cosmology and daily lives.

Within the Abzu's watery embrace, Enki exercises his role as a master engineer and architect of the cosmos, utilizing the fertile chaos of these primeval waters to fashion the world.

His actions within this domain are emblematic of the creative process itself, blending wisdom with the raw materials of existence to bring forth life and civilization. This space is not just a mythical location but a symbol of potentiality, where the waters await Enki's guiding hand to transform them into sources of fertility and prosperity for the land above. Through the mythos of the Abzu, the Sumerians expressed their understanding of the earth's hidden waterways, recognizing their critical importance in the emergence and maintenance of life.

The story of the Abzu and Enki's dominion over it weaves a narrative that is both cosmic and intimate, highlighting the essential role of water in the sustenance of both the earth and the human spirit. It speaks to the interconnectedness of all things, where the divine intermingles with the material and creation springs from the depths. Enki, in his mastery over the Abzu, serves as a guardian of these sacred waters, ensuring their flow nurtures the world. This depiction of Enki and the Abzu encapsulates a fundamental Mesopotamian belief in the sanctity of water, not just as a physical resource but as a divine gift, central to the unfolding of life and the continuation of civilization.

## ENGINEERING AND ARCHITECTURE

Enki's influence in the realms of engineering and architecture is a reflection of his profound understanding of order, structure, and the harmonious integration of form and function. As the deity responsible for bestowing humanity with the knowledge of building and design, Enki's contributions extend beyond the spiritual to the very foundations of Sumerian society. Through his guidance, the people learned to harness the natural world, constructing edifices that stood as a testament to their ingenuity and to the divine inspiration they received. This blending of practical skill with celestial wisdom underpins the monumental achievements of Sumerian architecture, from the majestic ziggurats that pierced the heavens to the intricate canal systems that transformed arid landscapes into fertile oases.

Enki's role as a divine engineer is most vividly illustrated in the mythological narratives that recount his feats of problem-solving and innovation. He is portrayed as a figure who, through a deep understanding of the natural laws, could avert disaster and promote prosperity. His interventions in the architectural and engineering challenges faced by the Sumerians are emblematic of the broader theme of divine assistance in human endeavors, highlighting the reciprocal relationship between the gods and their worshippers. In this light, Enki emerges not merely as a god of water but as a patron of all forms of creative expression and construction, encouraging the development of spaces that are in harmony with the divine order and the natural world.

The legacy of Enki in the fields of engineering and architecture is a testament to the enduring human quest for balance between the environment and our creations within it. His teachings, passed down through generations, inspired the Sumerians to pursue advancements that aligned with the cosmic order, ensuring their structures were not only functional but sacred. The principles of design and construction that Enki imparted to humanity reflect a holistic approach to architecture, one that integrates environmental awareness with aesthetic and spiritual considerations. Through Enki's guidance, the Sumerians were able to create a built environment that mirrored the complexity and beauty of the

ENKI AND THE WORLD ORDER

cosmos, establishing a model for future civilizations to follow.

## AGRICULTURE AND FERTILITY

Enki's mastery over the waters of the Abzu extended into the realms of agriculture and fertility, laying the groundwork for the prosperity of Sumerian civilization. His control over the life-giving rivers ensured that the fields were fertile, the granaries were full, and the people were nourished. This aspect of Enki's domain illustrates the intrinsic link between water, the source of all life, and the agricultural abundance that sustains civilizations. Through his benevolent manipulation of the waterways, Enki guaranteed the seasonal floods that replenished the soil, demonstrating the critical role of divine stewardship in the maintenance of earthly bounty.

The stories of Enki's interventions in agriculture are not just tales of divine benevolence; they are reflections on the symbiotic relationship between humans and the natural world. By teaching humanity the principles of irrigation, crop rotation, and soil management, Enki equipped them with the knowledge to work in harmony with the earth. This transfer of wisdom underscores a key theme in Mesopotamian mythology: the idea that prosperity is achieved through cooperation with the divine, adherence to celestial laws, and respect for the natural order. Enki's role in fostering agricultural fertility is a testament to his foresight and his commitment to the well-being of humanity, ensuring that the people could thrive in their environment.

The impact of Enki's contributions to agriculture and fertility resonates beyond the ancient fields of Sumer, echoing into the present as a reminder of our continued dependence on the natural world. The practices initiated under his guidance are a testament to the ingenuity of the Sumerians and their deep understanding of ecological balance. In Enki's stewardship of water and fertility, we find the roots of sustainable agriculture, a legacy that highlights the importance of wise resource management and environmental stewardship. Through these ancient narratives, Enki emerges as a figure of immense relevance, embodying the principles of sustainability and respect for the earth that are increasingly recognized as essential for the continuation of life and civilization.

## CRAFTS AND CREATIONS

Enki's influence extends into the realm of crafts and creations, where his ingenuity and wisdom sparked a revolution in Sumerian material culture. As the patron of artisans, Enki didn't just preside over the waters but flowed through the veins of society, infusing craftsmen with divine inspiration. This connection fostered an environment where artistry and innovation flourished, leading to advancements in metallurgy, ceramics, and textile production. These crafts were not mere occupations but sacred acts, imbued with spiritual significance and reflective of the society's deep respect for the creative process. Through Enki's guidance, the Sumerians came to understand craftsmanship as a dialogue between the mortal and the divine, a means of bringing celestial order into the tangible world.

The legacy of Enki in Sumerian crafts is evident in the exquisite artifacts that have survived to this day, each piece a testament to the skill and creativity of its maker. These items, ranging from intricately designed jewelry to robust

# ENKI AND THE WORLD ORDER

tools and weapons, speak volumes about the sophistication of Sumerian artisans and their ability to transform raw materials into objects of beauty and utility. Enki's hand guided this transformation, which was more than just a physical process; rather, it was a transmutation of the ordinary into the divine, a reflection of the god's own creative powers. Enki's patronage of the arts ensured that craftsmanship was held in high esteem, regarded as a vital component of civilization's progress, and a mirror of the cosmic order.

## MYTHS OF INVENTION AND INNOVATION

The myths surrounding Enki's role in invention and innovation are not merely accounts of divine intervention but narratives that underscore the importance of creativity and ingenuity in human development. These stories, rich with allegorical meaning, depict Enki as a figure who challenges the status quo, pushing the boundaries of what is known and possible. In these tales, Enki is often seen bestowing upon humanity the secrets of the gods, revealing the techniques and knowledge required to advance civilization. This act of transmission is symbolic of the Sumerians' belief in progress through divine wisdom, where each innovation is a step closer to understanding the mysteries of the universe.

Enki's adventures in these myths often involve overcoming obstacles through cleverness and technical skill, highlighting the god's association with problem-solving and creative thinking. Whether it's devising solutions to control the floodwaters or inventing the plow to ease the toil of agriculture, Enki's contributions are celebrated as milestones in the journey of human achievement. These narratives serve as inspirational tales that encourage exploration and experimentation, embodying the spirit of discovery that characterized Sumerian society. Through the figure of Enki, the Sumerians explored the potential for human ingenuity to mirror divine creativity, fostering a culture that revered innovation as a sacred pursuit.

## ENKI AS PATRON OF ARTISANS

Enki's role as the patron of artisans is a reflection of his broader significance as a deity of creation and wisdom. In this capacity, he embodies the ideals of craftsmanship, innovation, and artistic expression, inspiring those who craft and create to strive for excellence. Artisans, under Enki's patronage, were not mere laborers but esteemed members of society, their skills regarded as gifts from the divine. This reverence for the act of creation established a culture in which art and craftsmanship were seen as vital expressions of the human condition, ways of connecting with the divine, and bringing beauty and function into the world.

The relationship between Enki and the artisans of Sumer is emblematic of the symbiotic relationship between the divine and the mortal realms. Through this partnership, the material world is continuously renewed and enriched, reflecting the dynamism and creativity of the cosmos. Enki's influence ensures that the work of artisans is more than just the production of goods; it is a sacred act that celebrates the creative potential inherent in all of us. This acknowledgment of craftsmanship as a divine endeavor highlights the Mesopotamian understanding of art as a medium of communication with the gods, a form of worship that beautifies the world and elevates the spirit.

## WATER AS A SYMBOL OF LIFE AND KNOWLEDGE

In the figure of Enki, water transcends its physical properties to become a symbol of life, knowledge, and renewal. As the god of the sweet waters of the Abzu, Enki's domain over this vital resource positions him as a key figure in the sustenance and advancement of civilization. Water, in this context, is not merely a necessity for survival but a metaphor for the flow of wisdom and the growth of society. The Sumerians recognized the dual nature of water—its capacity to nurture and destroy—and in Enki, they saw the embodiment of this duality, a deity who harnesses the chaotic potential of water to benefit the world.

This symbolism extends to the way Sumerians viewed knowledge and wisdom, often depicted as flowing from Enki like water from a source. Just as water carves through stone and brings life to barren lands, so does knowledge, when Enki imparts it, have the power to transform societies and individuals. This conceptualization of water as a bearer of life and wisdom underscores the profound respect the Sumerians held for this element and its divine steward. Through the myths and legends of Enki, water becomes more than a resource; it is a sacred element, a conduit for divine grace, and a symbol of the endless cycle of creation and discovery that drives the universe.

# ENKI AND THE GODS: RELATIONSHIPS AND RIVALRIES

## ENKI AND AN: FATHER AND SON DYNAMICS

The relationship between Enki and An, the sky god, encapsulates a complex dynamic that is both emblematic of divine hierarchy and reflective of the nuanced father-son relationships observed in human societies. An, as the supreme deity of the Sumerian pantheon, represents authority and the overarching order of the cosmos, while Enki, his son, embodies wisdom, water, and life's creative forces. This relationship is not one of mere subservience; rather, it is a partnership where respect is mutual and influence is reciprocal. Enki, despite his subordinate position, often acts as a counselor to An, offering insights that shape the very structure of the universe. This dynamic illustrates the balance between power and wisdom, authority and innovation, highlighting the Sumerians' appreciation for the complexities of familial and hierarchical relationships.

The interactions between Enki and An delve into themes of loyalty, duty, and the pursuit of harmony within the divine realm. Their collaboration in the cosmic order's maintenance demonstrates the importance of combining strength with wisdom and power with foresight. It is through this union of qualities that the gods manage to uphold the balance of the universe, ensuring its continued prosperity. Enki's role in this partnership is particularly significant, as it underscores the value of intelligence and creativity in resolving conflicts and fostering growth. This father-son dynamic, while divine in nature, serves as a mirror to the human experience, reflecting the intricate dance of respecting tradition while embracing change.

## ENKI AND NINHURSAG: CREATIVITY AND CONFLICT

The relationship between Enki and Ninhursag, the earth and mother goddess, is a testament to the intertwining of creativity and conflict in the process of creation. Their interactions, which reflect the complex relationship between the earth and water, are characterized by both cooperation and tension as deities in charge of various facets of life and nature. Ninhursag's fertility and Enki's waters are fundamental to life's flourishing, yet their union is not without its challenges. This dynamic speaks to the Sumerians' understanding of the natural world as a place of inherent contradiction, where creation often arises from the resolution of conflict. The myths surrounding Enki and Ninhursag explore themes of regeneration, healing, and the cyclical nature of life, emphasizing the necessity of balance and reconciliation in the face of discord.

Enki and Ninhursag navigate the delicate balance between creation and destruction, order and chaos, in the stories of their encounters. Their relationship, which experienced moments of conflict and then reconciliation, exemplifies the Sumerians' faith in the transformative potential of conflict. Through their interactions, the gods demonstrate that creativity often emerges from the resolution of tension, a lesson that resonates beyond the mythic realm into the realm of human creativity and innovation. Enki's relationship with Ninhursag, while fraught with challenges, ultimately reinforces the notion that harmony is achieved not through the avoidance of conflict but through its constructive resolution.

ENKI AND INANNA: THE TRANSFER OF THE ME

The narrative of Enki and Inanna, involving the transfer of the Me, is rich with symbolism and insight into the dynamics of power, wisdom, and the quest for autonomy. Inanna, the goddess of love and war, seeks to acquire the Me from Enki, aiming to bring knowledge and civilization to her city of Uruk. This story highlights the themes of ambition, cunning, and the desire for empowerment, showcasing a moment where divine entities engage in a complex interplay of negotiation and strategy. Enki, initially reluctant to part with the Me, eventually acquiesces, a decision that underscores the importance of knowledge sharing and the diffusion of divine gifts for the greater good of civilization. This tale is not just a mythic account of rivalry but a profound exploration of the conditions under which wisdom and power are transferred and transformed.

The relationship between Enki and Inanna, in this context, transcends the personal, reflecting broader themes of governance, stewardship, and the responsibilities that come with divine power. Inanna's determination to secure the Me for her people and Enki's eventual willingness to support her endeavor illustrate the dynamic nature of divine authority and the role of wisdom in fostering societal progress. This narrative serves as a metaphor for the evolution of societies, highlighting the necessity of innovation, the value of assertiveness, and the importance of wisdom in navigating the path to advancement. Through the lens of this myth, the Sumerians convey a timeless message about the power of ambition, tempered by wisdom, and the transformative potential of knowledge when it is shared for the common good.

## ENKI AND THE UNDERWORLD

Enki's journey into the underworld presents a fascinating glimpse into the Sumerian conception of the afterlife and the gods' role in mediating between the realms of the living and the dead. This voyage is not merely a descent into darkness but a mission of balance and restoration, highlighting Enki's responsibilities beyond the waters and crafts. The underworld, a domain of mystery and finality, becomes a stage for Enki's wisdom and diplomatic skill as he navigates its challenges to ensure the continuity of life and death. This narrative explores the themes of sacrifice, redemption, and the cyclical nature of existence, emphasizing the interconnectedness of all realms in the Sumerian cosmos.

In his interactions with the deities of the underworld, Enki exemplifies the qualities of a mediator, striving to uphold harmony and prevent conflict from disrupting the cosmic order. His journey is a testament to the Sumerians' belief in the necessity of a balance between the forces of life and death, creation and dissolution. Through Enki's endeavors in the underworld, the myth communicates a profound understanding of the universe as a place of eternal cycles, where endings are precursors to new beginnings. This story, rich with allegorical depth, serves as a reminder of the constant flux of existence and the role of wisdom and courage in facing the unknown.

## DIPLOMACY AND DECEPTION

Enki's use of diplomacy and deception stands out in the intricate web of divine relationships as a testament to his complex character and the nuanced nature of divine interaction. His diplomatic efforts are often aimed at maintaining harmony among the gods and resolving conflicts with a blend of wisdom, persuasion, and strategic foresight. Yet, Enki is also known for his cunning, employing deception as a tool to achieve greater ends, whether to protect humanity, secure resources, or balance power among the deities. This duality in Enki's approach highlights the Sumerian understanding of leadership and governance, where skillful negotiation and the occasional ruse are both essential in the art of divine and mortal politics.

Enki's mastery of diplomacy and deception is not an endorsement of deceit for its own sake but a recognition of its value in navigating complex political landscapes. Through his actions, Enki embodies the principle that the path to harmony often requires flexibility, creativity, and a deep understanding of the motivations of friends and foes alike. These tales, while set in the realm of gods, reflect the Sumerians' own experiences with the challenges of leadership and the importance of strategic thinking in the preservation of order and the advancement of society.

## SIBLING RIVALRY: ENKI AND ENLIL

The dynamic between Enki and his brother Enlil, the god of air and storm, encapsulates the tension between order and chaos, innovation and tradition. As siblings, their rivalry is not just a personal contention but a cosmic duel that shapes the fate of the universe and humanity. Enlil, with his command over the winds and the weather, represents the raw power of nature and the necessity of order. At the same time, Enki symbolizes the potential for creativity and change with his dominion over the waters and wisdom. This rivalry, though fraught with conflict, is also a source of growth and balance, as the two gods' opposing forces drive the evolution of the world and the development of civilization.

This sibling rivalry is a narrative that explores the complexity of power, the challenges of governance, and the balance required to sustain life and civilization. Through their conflicts and reconciliations, Enki and Enlil demonstrate the necessity of both stability and adaptability, underscoring the Sumerians' belief in the value of diversity in divine governance. Their interactions remind us that progress often emerges from the tension between competing ideas and forces, a lesson that resonates in the realm of human affairs as much as it does in the divine.

## PATRON OF HUMANITY VS. DIVINE AUTHORITY

Enki stands out from other gods because he is the patron of humanity, which frequently puts him at odds with other gods' claims to divine power. His commitment to the welfare of humans, demonstrated through his efforts to impart knowledge, mediate conflicts, and ensure prosperity, underscores a fundamental aspect of his deity: the belief in the potential of humanity to reflect the divine. This stance, however, frequently places Enki in a delicate position as he navigates the fine line between supporting human advancement and challenging the established divine order. His advocacy for humanity is not just an act of rebellion but a reflection of his understanding of the interconnectedness of all beings and the importance of nurturing the divine spark within mankind.

This dynamic between Enki's patronage and the broader divine authority explores themes of compassion, innovation, and the quest for balance in the governance of the cosmos. Enki's actions, driven by a deep love for humanity and a belief in its capacities, often require him to employ both wisdom and deception to achieve his ends. Through these narratives, the Sumerians articulated a vision of the divine that is actively involved in the human world, not as distant rulers but as participants in the ongoing project of creation and civilization. Enki's relationship with humanity, which is characterized by goodness and a desire to uplift, serves as a potent reminder of the potential for cooperation between the mortal and the divine, a cooperation that is necessary for the flourishing of both realms.

# ENKI'S OFFSPRING: THE PANTHEON EXPANDS

## MARDUK: RISE OF A GOD

Marduk's ascension within the pantheon is a tale of power, cunning, and the complexities of divine politics. As the son of Enki, Marduk inherited a rich legacy of wisdom and strength, qualities that would propel him to prominence among the gods. His rise to power was not merely a function of his lineage but a testament to his ability to navigate the turbulent waters of divine rivalry and ambition. Marduk's journey from a god among many to the king of the gods encapsulates the fluid dynamics of power within the Mesopotamian divine order, reflecting the Sumerians' nuanced understanding of leadership and authority.

The story of Marduk is particularly significant for its role in the Babylonian Enuma Elish, where he leads the gods in battle against the chaos monster Tiamat, securing his position as the supreme deity. This epic victory not only cements

Marduk's status but also symbolizes the triumph of order over chaos, a theme central to Mesopotamian mythology. Through Marduk, Enki's wisdom and resourcefulness find their fullest expression, showcasing the ability of the next generation to surpass their predecessors and shape the destiny of the cosmos.

Marduk's rise reflects the evolving nature of the Mesopotamian pantheon, where gods ascend in power and prominence through their deeds and the devotion of their followers. His story, interwoven with themes of struggle, triumph, and the responsibility of power, offers insights into the Mesopotamian worldview, where the divine order is both dynamic and reflective of the society's values and aspirations. Marduk's legacy, rooted in his relationship with Enki, serves as a powerful narrative of divine leadership, emphasizing the importance of wisdom, strength, and the continual quest for balance within the universe.

### NINGIZZIDA: GUARDIAN OF THE GATE

Ningizzida, another of Enki's offspring, occupies a unique position as the guardian of the heavenly gate, a role that underscores the interconnectedness of the cosmos and the underworld. His guardianship is not just a matter of protecting divine realms but also of maintaining the balance between the different worlds, a responsibility that echoes Enki's own role as a mediator and keeper of cosmic order. Ningizzida's presence at the gates symbolizes the transition between life and death, the earthly and the divine, highlighting the Mesopotamian belief in the cyclical nature of existence and the continuity of life beyond death.

This deity's association with serpents and the dragon, symbols of rebirth and healing, further accentuates his role as a bridge between worlds. Ningizzida's attributes reflect the Mesopotamians' complex understanding of the divine as multifaceted beings who embody various aspects of the natural and spiritual realms. Through Ningizzida, Enki's legacy of wisdom and protection is manifested in the stewardship of the thresholds of existence, ensuring the smooth passage of souls and the maintenance of cosmic harmony.

Ningizzida's role within the pantheon and his functions as guardian highlight the importance of gatekeepers in Mesopotamian mythology, serving as protectors of sacred knowledge and order. His position at the heavenly gate is evidence of the gods' faith in him, which stems from his lineage and his demonstrated wisdom. Through Ningizzida, the themes of guardianship, transition, and the cyclical journey of the soul are explored, offering a nuanced perspective on the Mesopotamian conception of the afterlife and the eternal responsibilities of the gods.

### DUMUZID: THE SHEPHERD KING

Dumuzid, the shepherd king, embodies the pastoral and agricultural aspects of Mesopotamian society, reflecting the deep connection between the divine and the agrarian cycle. As one of Enki's offspring, Dumuzid's role transcends the mere oversight of flocks and fields; he becomes a symbol of fertility, renewal, and the sustenance of life. His kingship is not limited to the earthly realm but extends into the divine, where he participates in the sacred marriage with Inanna, linking the agricultural cycles with the rhythms of the cosmos. This union, celebrated in myth and ritual, reinforces the Mesopotamian belief in the harmony between heaven and earth, the divine and the mortal.

Tragic events also occur in Dumuzid's story, as his descent into the underworld and subsequent seasonal return parallel the planting and harvesting cycle. This mythological motif of death and rebirth is central to Mesopotamian religion, symbolizing the eternal struggle between life and death, growth and decay. Dumuzid's journey through the underworld and his eventual return to the land of the living are reflective of the agricultural beliefs of the time, embodying the hope for renewal and the resilience of life in the face of adversity.

As a deity, Dumuzid serves as a bridge between the people and the gods, his life and trials echoing the human experience of loss, hope, and the perpetual cycle of renewal. His connection to Enki and the broader divine narrative emphasizes the role of the gods in the everyday lives of the Mesopotamians, their myths providing comfort and explanation for the mysteries of existence. Through Dumuzid, Enki's influence on the natural world and its cycles is celebrated, showcasing the intricate relationship between divine providence, kingship, and the fertility of the earth.

### NANSHE: GODDESS OF SOCIAL JUSTICE

Nanshe, who is celebrated for her wisdom and compassion, holds a distinctive place among Enki's offspring as the goddess of social justice, orphans, and the downtrodden. Her domain extends beyond the spiritual, touching the lives of the most vulnerable in society and advocating for fairness and equality. Nanshe's role underscores the Mesopotamians' recognition of the gods' responsibility not just for the cosmic

ENKI AND THE WORLD ORDER

order but for the moral and social order as well. Her festivals, particularly the New Year's purification and the assessment of dreams, were occasions for communal reflection on justice, social obligations, and the divine mandate to care for one another.

Her priesthood, known for its role in divination and interpretation of omens, served as intermediaries between Nanshe and her people, guiding the community through her wisdom. This connection between deity and devotee highlights the active engagement of the gods in the daily affairs of humanity, reinforcing the belief in a cosmos where divine justice and human society are intimately linked. Nanshe's dedication to social justice, especially in her support for those without voice or power, reflects the Sumerians' complex understanding of divinity, where gods are not only creators and destroyers but also protectors and nurturers of their people.

The mythological significance of Nanshe and her emphasis on social justice offer a glimpse into the values and ethics that underpinned Sumerian society. Through her, Enki's legacy of wisdom and guardianship is manifested in the pursuit of a just and equitable society, illustrating the belief that the divine order should mirror the moral order. Nanshe's role as a champion for the marginalized showcases the Mesopotamians' sophisticated conception of justice, where the well-being of the individual is seen as integral to the health of the community and the favor of the gods.

## DIVINE DYNASTIES AND LEGACIES

The offspring of Enki, each embodying different aspects of the cosmos, illustrate the breadth of Enki's influence across the pantheon and the natural world. These divine children, from Marduk to Nanshe, represent the continuation of Enki's legacy, their roles and stories weaving a complex tapestry of mythology that reflects the Mesopotamians' understanding of the universe. The pantheon, with its myriad deities, serves as a mirror to the society from which it sprang, embodying the values, fears, and aspirations of the Mesopotamian people. Through these divine dynasties, the Sumerians explored themes of power, wisdom, justice, and the cycles of life and death, embedding their religious beliefs with the richness of their cultural and environmental experiences.

The legacy of Enki and his offspring is not confined to the annals of mythology but extends into the very structure of Mesopotamian civilization. The gods' roles in agriculture, justice, craft, and kingship reflect the interconnectedness of religion and daily life, where the divine order shapes the social order. This blending of the celestial and the terrestrial highlights the Mesopotamians' belief in a cosmos where humans and gods share a common destiny, their fates intertwined in the ongoing project of creation and civilization. Through the stories of Enki's children, the Sumerians articulated a vision of a world rich with divine presence, where each deity plays a role in maintaining balance and advancing society.

## THE ROLE OF OFFSPRING IN ENKI'S WORLD ORDER

Enki's children, each with their own unique domains and responsibilities, play critical roles in the maintenance of the cosmic and social order. Their actions, whether in the heavens, the earth, or the underworld, are extensions of Enki's will, contributing to the balance and harmony of the universe. These deities, through their governance of various aspects of the natural and human worlds, embody the principles of their father, from the nurturing of life to the dispensation of wisdom and justice. The role of Enki's offspring in the world order is a testament to the depth of Enki's influence, his creativity, and his foresight manifested in the diversity and capability of his divine progeny.

The participation of these gods in the affairs of the cosmos and humanity underscores the dynamic nature of the Sumerian divine order, where change and continuity are constant themes. Through their endeavors, Enki's children ensure the perpetuation of the cycles of life, the progression of civilization, and the upholding of cosmic law. Their interactions with humans, ranging from the provision of fertility and sustenance to the administration of justice, highlight the reciprocal relationship between the divine and the mortal, a core aspect of Mesopotamian spirituality.

## MYTHOLOGICAL SIGNIFICANCE OF ENKI'S CHILDREN

The mythological narratives surrounding Enki's offspring serve multiple functions within Sumerian culture, acting as vehicles for theological exploration, moral instruction, and cosmological speculation. Through the tales of Marduk, Ningizzida, Dumuzid, and Nanshe, the Sumerians engaged with questions of power, responsibility, and the nature of the divine. These stories, rich in symbolic meaning, provided a framework through which the complexities of the human condition could be examined and understood. The significance of Enki's children in mythology is profound, offering insights into the Sumerian worldview, where the divine is intimately involved in the shaping of human destiny.

These narratives, with their gods who embody various facets of existence, reflect the Sumerians' deep reverence for the natural world and their keen awareness of the moral and ethical dimensions of life. Through the deeds and trials of Enki's progeny, the Mesopotamians explored the virtues of wisdom, justice, creativity, and compassion, weaving a rich tapestry of belief that informed their practices and understanding of the world. The mythological significance of Enki's children lies in their ability to bridge the celestial and the earthly, bringing the divine into the every day and highlighting the indelible link between the gods and their human worshippers.

# ENKI AND HUMANITY: CREATOR, SAVIOR, AND TRICKSTER

## THE CREATION OF HUMANKIND

The Creation of Humankind is a tale that sits at the heart of Enki's relationship with the mortal world, showcasing his role not just as a creator but as a nurturer and protector. According to Mesopotamian mythology, it was Enki who, recognizing the gods' need for rest from their labors, proposed the creation of humans to carry the burden of work. This act of creation was more than a mere delegation of duties; it was the inception of a profound relationship between the divine and the human. Enki's hand in molding the first humans from the clay of the earth imbues humanity with a divine spark, setting the stage for a complex interplay of dependence, reverence, and cooperation that would define the cosmic order.

This narrative of human creation highlights Enki's compassion and foresight, traits that underscore his benevolence towards humanity. Unlike other gods, who might have viewed humans solely as servants, Enki saw them as partners in the stewardship of the earth. His desire to unite the divine and the human, to infuse the physical world with the spirit of the heavens, was what motivated him to create humankind. This act of creation, then, is not just about the origins of humans but about the establishment of a covenant between Enki and humanity, a bond that is both sacred and essential for the balance of the cosmos.

### THE FLOOD MYTH: ENKI'S WARNING

The flood myth, with Enki at its center, is a narrative that resonates with themes of salvation, foresight, and the complex relationship between divine will and human destiny. In this story, Enki, aware of the other gods' decision to send a flood to cleanse the earth, chooses to warn Utnapishtim, thus saving humanity from certain destruction. This act of defiance is not merely a rebellion against the divine consensus but a demonstration of Enki's commitment to his creations. By providing Utnapishtim with the knowledge to build an ark, Enki ensures the survival of humans and animals alike, preserving the life he had a hand in creating.

Enki's intervention in the flood myth is symbolic of his role as a savior, a deity willing to challenge the pantheon's decrees for humanity's sake. This story highlights the dual nature of the divine, capable of both wrath and mercy, and positions Enki as a mediator between these extremes. His actions underscore the belief that wisdom and compassion can avert disaster, providing a way forward even in the face of overwhelming odds. Through the flood myth, Enki's relationship with humanity is deepened, cementing his status as a protector and reinforcing the bond between the creator and the created.

## ENKI'S GIFTS TO HUMANITY

Beyond the act of creation, Enki's contributions to humanity are manifold, encompassing the realms of knowledge, culture, and the arts. He is depicted as a benefactor who bestowed upon humans the gifts of writing, agriculture, law, and the crafts and tools that enabled the rise of civilization and the flourishing of Sumerian society. These gifts were not mere acts of divine largesse but deliberate interventions meant to empower humans and provide them with the means to shape their destiny and mirror the divine order on earth. Enki's role in this transfer of knowledge is central to understanding his relationship with humanity, highlighting his desire to see his creations thrive and evolve.

Enki's generosity in sharing the secrets of the gods with humans illustrates his unique position within the pantheon as a deity deeply invested in the material world. His actions reflect a profound understanding of the potential within humanity to reflect the complexity and beauty of the divine. This relationship between Enki and humans, marked by the sharing of sacred knowledge, underscores the Sumerian belief in the possibility of harmony between the heavenly and the earthly. Through Enki's gifts, humanity was able to transcend its mortal limitations, embracing a divine heritage that continues to inspire and guide.

## THE TRICKSTER GOD: MYTHS AND LEGENDS

In the tapestry of Mesopotamian mythology, Enki occupies a special place as the trickster god, a figure whose cunning and wit challenge the status quo and introduce change. His trickery is not born of malice but serves as a catalyst for growth, innovation, and the resolution of conflict. The legends surrounding Enki's exploits, from outsmarting fellow gods to bending cosmic laws, are imbued with humor and wisdom, revealing the multifaceted nature of his character. These stories not only entertain but also convey deep truths about the world, illustrating the value of cleverness and adaptability in overcoming obstacles.

Enki's role as a trickster highlights his mastery over language, diplomacy, and strategy, qualities that allow him to navigate the complex dynamics of the divine realm. His actions often result in beneficial outcomes for humanity, demonstrating his commitment to the welfare of his creations. Through these mythological narratives, Enki emerges as a figure who embodies the power of intelligence over brute force, a lesson that resonates with the human experience. The trickster motif, with Enki at its center, serves as a reminder of the transformative potential of wit and the importance of viewing challenges from multiple perspectives.

## ENKI'S ROLE AS MEDIATOR

Within the celestial hierarchy, Enki's capacity to act as a mediator is unparalleled, stemming from his deep reservoir of wisdom and his understanding of the intricate balance that governs the cosmos. His interventions in disputes among the gods and between the divine and the mortal realms are characterized by a keen sense of justice and a desire to maintain harmony. Enki's mediation is not merely a matter of resolving conflicts but of preserving the cosmic order, ensuring that the universe remains a place where life can thrive. This role underscores the Sumerians' belief in the necessity of balance and the value of wisdom in achieving it.

Enki's mediation extends beyond the resolution of divine quarrels to the guidance he provides to humanity, helping them navigate the challenges of existence. Through his teachings and interventions, Enki bridges the gap between the gods and humans, fostering a relationship based on mutual respect and understanding. His role as a mediator highlights the interconnectedness of all things, reinforcing the idea that harmony within the cosmos is a collective responsibility. Through Enki's efforts, the divine and the mortal are woven together in a delicate tapestry of existence, where each thread is essential to the whole.

## WISDOM, MAGIC, AND THE OCCULT

Enki's dominion also extends into the realms of wisdom, magic, and the occult, areas where his influence has profound implications for the understanding and manipulation of the natural and supernatural worlds. His expertise in these esoteric arts is a boon to humanity, offering protection, insight, and the ability to commune with the divine. Under Enki's patronage, the practice of magic and the pursuit of occult knowledge are seen as sacred endeavors, ways to align one's will with the cosmic order and enact change according to divine principles. This aspect of Enki's character emphasizes the Mesopotamians' appreciation for the unseen forces that shape their world and their belief in the power of knowledge to harness these forces for the benefit of society.

The teachings and spells attributed to Enki form the foundation of Mesopotamian magical practice, imbuing priests and practitioners with the wisdom to heal, protect, and be divine. This legacy of occult knowledge passed down through generations serves as a testament to Enki's lasting impact on the spiritual and intellectual lives of the Sumerians. Through his guidance, the mysteries of the cosmos are made accessible, and the boundaries between the human and the divine are blurred. Enki's mastery over magic and the occult highlights the Sumerians' belief in the practical application of divine wisdom, where spirituality and daily life are intimately connected.

## THE ENDURING BOND BETWEEN ENKI AND HUMANS

The bond between Enki and humanity is a central theme in Sumerian mythology, reflecting a relationship that is both nurturing and complex. Enki's role as creator, savior, and teacher establishes him as a pivotal figure in the lives of humans, a god whose influence permeates every aspect of their existence. This enduring bond is characterized by a mutual dependency: humans rely on Enki for guidance and protection, while Enki finds purpose in the flourishing of his creations. Through the myths and legends that recount his deeds, Enki is portrayed as a deity deeply invested in the human experience, committed to fostering growth, creativity, and understanding among his mortal charges.

This relationship, however, is not without its challenges. Enki's trickster nature and his occasional demands on humanity test the strength and resilience of this bond. Yet, even in moments of conflict, the underlying affection and respect between Enki and humans remain evident, symbolizing the potential for reconciliation and the continuation of their shared journey. The enduring bond between Enki and humanity is a testament to the Mesopotamians' belief in the benevolence of the gods and their role in guiding and shaping human destiny. The Sumerians celebrated the complexities and joys of life in a world where the whims of the gods prevailed through Enki as they probed the depths of this divine-human relationship.

# SACRED SITES AND CULT CENTERS

## ERIDU: THE FIRST CITY

Eridu, often hailed as the first city of the ancient world, stands as a testament to the profound impact of Enki on Mesopotamian civilization. Situated at the edge of what was once the Persian Gulf, this city was believed to be the earthly abode of Enki, where the god's presence permeated every brick and filled the air with the essence of the divine. The significance of Eridu extends beyond its architectural marvels; it represents the dawn of urban life, a place where humanity first gathered to live under the auspices of a god. This convergence of the divine and the mortal in Eridu illustrates the Sumerians' deep connection to their deities, viewing their cities not just as places of habitation but as sacred spaces where the gods walked among them.

The foundation of Eridu is steeped in mythology, with Enki himself credited with its creation. According to legend, it was here that Enki brought forth the sweet waters from the earth, allowing life to flourish in an otherwise barren landscape. This act of creation is symbolic of Enki's role as a nurturer and protector, showcasing his benevolence and pivotal role in sustaining life. Eridu's emergence as a center of worship and civilization underlines the central belief in the gods' active involvement in human affairs, a theme that resonates throughout Mesopotamian history. The city's development from a modest settlement to a thriving urban center mirrors the growth of Mesopotamian society, reflecting the advancements in culture, technology, and spirituality that characterized the era.

## THE E-ABZU TEMPLE

At the heart of Eridu lay the E-Abzu, a temple dedicated to Enki, marking the physical and spiritual center of the city. This temple, more than a mere structure of worship, was a symbol of the cosmic order, a sacred space that connected the heavens and the earth. The architecture of the E-Abzu, with its intricate design and alignment with celestial bodies, reflects the Sumerians' sophisticated understanding of the universe and their desire to harmonize their spiritual practices with the rhythms of the cosmos. The temple served as a focal point for the community, a place where the divine and the human realms intersected, allowing for communication with the gods and the enactment of rituals that ensured the city's prosperity and protection.

The significance of the E-Abzu extends beyond its architectural and religious importance; it represents the enduring legacy of Enki's teachings and his influence on Mesopotamian culture. The temple was not only a site of worship but also a center of learning, where priests and scholars gathered to study the mysteries of the divine and the natural world. This blend of spirituality and scholarship within the walls of the E-Abzu underscores the holistic approach the Sumerians took toward their gods, viewing them as sources of wisdom and guidance. Through the rituals and ceremonies performed in the temple, the inhabitants of Eridu sought to maintain the balance of the cosmos, a reflection of their belief in the interconnectedness of all aspects of existence.

## SACRED GEOGRAPHY: NIPPUR AND URUK

The sacred geography of Mesopotamia extends beyond Eridu, with cities like Nippur and Uruk playing pivotal roles in the spiritual landscape of the region. Nippur, regarded as the religious center of Sumer, housed the E-Kur, the temple of Enlil, Enki's brother, establishing a divine axis that balanced the powers of water and air, fertility, and storm. Uruk, on the other hand, was the seat of Inanna's worship, a city that epitomized the cultural and religious dynamism of Mesopotamian society. These cities, with their grand temples and elaborate rituals, were not mere points on a map but embodiments of the divine order, each contributing to the tapestry of sacred geography that defined the spiritual world of the Sumerians.

This network of sacred sites, interconnected through myths, trade routes, and pilgrimage paths, created a cohesive religious identity among the city-states of Mesopotamia. The centrality of these sites in the lives of the people underscored the importance of place in their understanding of the divine, with each city reflecting a different facet of the gods' personalities and powers. The significance of Nippur and Uruk, alongside Eridu, in the sacred geography of Mesopotamia highlights the complex relationship between the divine, the natural, and the human realms, a relationship that was mediated through the physical and spiritual landscapes of these ancient cities.

## PILGRIMAGE AND WORSHIP PRACTICES

Pilgrimage and worship practices in ancient Mesopotamia were deeply intertwined with the sacred geography of the land, with devotees traveling vast distances to pay homage at the temples of Enki, Enlil, Inanna, and other gods. These journeys were not merely religious obligations but acts of faith that connected individuals to the divine narrative of the cosmos. The act of pilgrimage, traversing the land to reach these sacred sites, was a physical manifestation of the spiritual quest for understanding, guidance, and blessing from the gods. Through these practices, the Sumerians sought to align themselves with the cosmic order to ensure the fertility of their crops, the prosperity of their cities, and the health of their communities.

The rituals performed at these temples, from offerings and sacrifices to hymns and prayers, were designed to maintain the balance between the human and divine realms. These ceremonies allowed for direct communication with the gods, a way to express gratitude, seek forgiveness, and petition for divine favor. The complexity and diversity of these worship practices reflect the Sumerians' deep reverence for the gods and their belief in the efficacy of rituals to influence the course of human destiny. Through these acts of devotion, the Mesopotamians reinforced the bonds between themselves and the deities they worshipped, ensuring the continuation of the divine order that sustained their world.

## ARCHAEOLOGICAL DISCOVERIES

The archaeological discoveries of sacred sites and cult centers in Mesopotamia have provided invaluable insights into the religious life of the ancient Sumerians. Excavations at Eridu, Nippur, Uruk, and other cities have uncovered the remnants of temples, altars, and ritual objects, offering a tangible connection to the spiritual world of the past. These findings, from cuneiform tablets recounting myths and hymns to artifacts used in worship, paint a vivid picture of the religious practices and beliefs that shaped Mesopotamian civilization. The archaeologists' discoveries of Sumerian material culture emphasize the significance of sacred sites as centers of communal identity and spiritual practice, demonstrating the importance of religion in the Sumerians' lives.

The study of these archaeological sites has also shed light on the evolution of Mesopotamian religion, tracing the development of the pantheon and the changing patterns of worship over time. Through the layers of history excavated at these sites, scholars have been able to reconstruct the complex relationship between the gods and their worshippers, gaining a deeper understanding of the role of religion in the formation of Mesopotamian society. The legacy of these sacred sites, preserved through the work of archaeologists, continues to inform our understanding of the ancient world, bridging the gap between the past and the present.

## THE SPREAD OF ENKI'S CULT

The cult of Enki, with its origins in the ancient city of Eridu, spread throughout Mesopotamia, influencing religious practices and beliefs across the region. This diffusion of Enki's worship was not a simple expansion of a cult but a complex process of integration and adaptation, reflecting the dynamic nature of Mesopotamian religion. As the cult of Enki encountered local deities and practices, it evolved, incorporating elements of these traditions while maintaining the core attributes of Enki as a god of wisdom, water, and creation. This syncretism illustrates the Mesopotamians' openness to religious diversity and their ability to find common ground among the myriad deities of their pantheon.

The spread of Enki's cult also highlights the god's appeal to a wide range of worshippers, from kings and priests to farmers and artisans. Enki's association with creation, fertility, and wisdom resonated with the fundamental concerns of ancient Mesopotamian society, ensuring his relevance across different cities and periods. The enduring popularity of Enki's cult can be attributed to the deity's multifaceted nature, his role as a protector and benefactor of humanity, and the practical and spiritual support his worship provided to the people. Through the cult of Enki, the Sumerians expressed their deepest aspirations and fears, finding in the god a reflection of their own complex relationship with the world.

## LEGACY OF SACRED SITES

The legacy of the sacred sites dedicated to Enki and other deities in Mesopotamia extends far beyond the ancient world, influencing contemporary understandings of spirituality, community, and the human relationship with the divine. These locations served as places of worship and pilgrimage, but they also served as metaphors for the Mesopotamians' search for connection, meaning, and order in a world under the control of forces they were unable to control. The enduring fascination with these ancient temples and cities speaks to the universal human desire to comprehend the cosmos and find our place within it. Through the study of these sacred sites, modern seekers can glimpse the profound spirituality of the Sumerians, a people for whom the divine was an integral part of the natural and social order.

The archaeological exploration of these sites has not only enriched our historical knowledge but has also provided a bridge to the past, allowing us to engage with the spiritual life of ancient Mesopotamia in a tangible way. The ruins of temples and cities stand as silent witnesses to the depth of religious feeling and the complexity of divine-human relations that characterized Sumerian civilization. In the legacy of these sacred sites, we find a reflection of our own search for the sacred, a reminder of the enduring power of faith and ritual to bind communities together and connect us with the divine. Through the study and preservation of these ancient places, we honor the spiritual heritage of Mesopotamia, carrying forward the legacy of Enki and the pantheon of gods who shaped the cradle of civilization.

# ENKI'S ADVERSARIES AND ALLIES

## THE ANUNNAKI ASSEMBLY

The Anunnaki Assembly serves as the cosmic council, a place of deliberation and decision-making where the destinies of gods and humans intertwine. Enki emerges as a voice of wisdom and moderation within this celestial gathering, often navigating the tumultuous dynamics of divine politics with astuteness and foresight. This gathering is more than just a platform for the gods; it also serves as a reflection of the Sumerian understanding of the universe as a place where conflict and agreement coexist, mirroring the complexity of their own societal structures. Through the interactions within the Anunnaki Assembly, Enki's role as mediator and innovator is highlighted, showcasing his ability to influence outcomes and guide the divine collective toward harmony and balance.

The dynamics of the Anunnaki Assembly reveal the nuanced relationships between the gods, characterized by alliances, rivalries, and the eternal quest for equilibrium. Enki's participation in this assembly underscores his commitment to the cosmic order, often bridging divides and offering solutions that benefit both the heavens and the earth. His actions within this divine council illustrate the Sumerians' belief in the power of diplomacy and dialogue, principles that underpin their own social and political systems. Through the prism of the Anunnaki Assembly, we glimpse the sophisticated nature of Sumerian theology, where gods embody the virtues and vices of humanity, engaging in debates and decisions that shape the fate of the world.

## ENKI VS. ENLIL: ORDER AND CHAOS

The dichotomy between Enki and Enlil, representing the forces of order and chaos, respectively, is a central theme in Mesopotamian mythology, encapsulating the dynamic tension that fuels the universe's ongoing creation and destruction. Enlil, as the god of air and storm, wields the power to bring both life-giving rains and devastating tempests, embodying the unpredictable nature of existence. In contrast, Enki, with his mastery over the waters and wisdom, stands as a symbol of order, fertility, and innovation. Their rivalry, while often manifesting in conflict, is also a source of growth and transformation, illustrating the necessity of balancing opposing forces to maintain the world's harmony and vitality.

This sibling rivalry transcends personal conflict, reflecting more profound philosophical questions about the nature of the universe and the role of the divine in human affairs. Through their interactions, Enki and Enlil engage in a cosmic dialogue about destiny, free will, and the moral responsibilities of power. The stories of their disputes and reconciliations serve as allegories for the Sumerians, teaching lessons about the importance of wisdom, the value of compromise, and the enduring quest for balance in a world defined by constant change. Through the lens of Enki and Enlil's relationship, we are invited to consider the complexities of leadership and the challenges of governance, both divine and mortal.

## ALLIANCES WITH GODDESSES

Enki's relationships with various goddesses highlight his role as a connector and collaborator within the divine realm, fostering alliances that extend his influence and enhance the cosmic order. His interactions with goddesses such as Ninhursag, the mother goddess, and Inanna, the goddess of love and war, reveal a deity capable of profound cooperation and mutual respect. These alliances are not merely strategic but are based on a shared commitment to the well-being of the world, reflecting Enki's understanding of the interconnectedness of all aspects of existence. Through his partnerships with these powerful deities, Enki demonstrates the importance of feminine wisdom and strength in the maintenance of balance and the promotion of growth within the cosmos.

The cooperation between Enki and these goddesses often results in the flourishing of life, the advancement of civilization, and the resolution of conflicts, underscoring the synergistic potential of divine collaboration. These relationships also illuminate the Sumerians' appreciation for the feminine divine, recognizing the critical roles that goddesses play in the creation and sustenance of life. Through the mythology surrounding Enki's alliances with goddesses, we are presented with a vision of a universe where harmony is achieved through collaboration, respect, and the blending of diverse powers and perspectives. This aspect of Enki's character not only highlights his diplomatic prowess but also celebrates the contributions of the goddesses to the cosmic order, showcasing the dynamic interplay of masculine and feminine energies in the shaping of destiny.

## DEMONS AND PROTECTIVE SPIRITS

In Sumerian mythology, Enki's domain is not limited to the benevolent aspects of the cosmos but also encompasses the darker, more mysterious forces. Among these are the demons and protective spirits that inhabit the world, entities over which Enki holds sway. His knowledge of the occult and magic enables him to command these beings, employing them as guardians of sacred spaces, protectors of humanity, or instruments of divine will. This control over the supernatural reflects Enki's mastery over all aspects of existence, from the life-giving waters to the shadowy realms inhabited by demons and spirits. It illustrates the complexity of his character, embodying the duality of creation, where light cannot exist without darkness and chaos constantly challenges order.

Enki's interactions with these beings highlight his role as a boundary-keeper, maintaining the balance between the seen and unseen worlds. The Sumerians believed in a universe filled with a variety of forces, both benevolent and malevolent, and his ability to navigate these realms and harness their powers for the benefit of the gods and humanity supports this belief. Through the mythology of demons and protective spirits, Enki is portrayed as a deity of unparalleled wisdom and power, capable of protecting the cosmic order from the forces of disorder. This aspect of Enki's deity serves as a reminder of the complexity of the world, where danger and protection are two sides of the same coin, and the knowledge to distinguish between them is the key to harmony and survival.

## COSMIC BATTLES AND BALANCE

The narrative of cosmic battles, with Enki often at the forefront, serves as a dramatic representation of the struggle to maintain balance in the universe. These battles, whether against chaotic forces personified by monsters or against the hubris of gods and humans alike, are emblematic of the constant tension that defines existence. Enki's involvement in these conflicts showcases his commitment to the cosmic order, wielding his wisdom and power to avert catastrophe and ensure the continuity of life. These stories are not merely tales of conflict but allegories for the challenges of governance and the responsibilities of power, reflecting the Sumerians' understanding of the universe as a place of inherent dynamism and fragility.

The role of adversaries in these mythological narratives is crucial, providing the opposition that necessitates the exercise of Enki's wisdom and strength. Through his confrontations with these forces, Enki embodies the qualities of a protector, a strategist, and a guardian of the cosmic order. The conclusion of these battles frequently results in a reaffirmation of the harmony between order and chaos, a theme that is consistent with the Sumerian conception of the world as a complex system subject to divine law. These cosmic battles, while fantastical, serve as metaphors for the real challenges faced by the Sumerians, from natural disasters to societal upheavals, illustrating the enduring human quest to find harmony in the midst of chaos.

## ENKI'S DIPLOMACY AND INFLUENCE

Enki's diplomacy and influence extend beyond the celestial realm, impacting the lives of humans and the course of history. His ability to mediate between conflicting forces, whether among the gods or between the divine and the mortal, highlights his role as a figure of immense wisdom and foresight. Through his diplomatic endeavors, Enki not only preserves the cosmic order but also fosters the conditions necessary for civilization's growth and prosperity. His influence is felt in the development of laws, the spread of knowledge, and the cultivation of the arts, marking him as a deity whose legacy is woven into the fabric of Mesopotamian culture.

Enki's role as a mediator is emblematic of the Sumerians' belief in the power of wisdom to resolve conflicts and guide the destiny of the cosmos. His interventions are characterized by a deep understanding of the complexities of the divine and human conditions, reflecting a nuanced approach to governance that values balance, compassion, and innovation. Through the mythology surrounding Enki's diplomacy and influence, we are presented with a vision of leadership that transcends the mere exercise of power, embodying the ideals of stewardship, cooperation, and mutual respect. This aspect of Enki's character serves as a reminder of the potential for leadership to effect positive change, inspiring future generations to seek harmony in their interactions with the world.

## THE ROLE OF ADVERSARIES IN MYTHOLOGY

The presence of adversaries in Mesopotamian mythology, particularly in the stories surrounding Enki, serves a critical function, acting as catalysts for growth, change, and the reaffirmation of cosmic and moral order. These antagonistic forces challenge Enki and the other gods, prompting them to demonstrate their wisdom, strength, and commitment to the well-being of the universe. The conflicts that arise from these confrontations are not mere obstacles but opportunities for the display of divine virtues and the exercise of celestial authority. Through these trials, the gods, with Enki at the forefront, navigate the complexities of their relationships and the responsibilities of their power, illustrating the dynamic nature of the cosmos.

The role of adversaries in these narratives underscores the Sumerian understanding of the world as a place of inherent conflict and resolution, where harmony is achieved through the balance of opposing forces. While fantastical, these mythological conflicts mirror the real challenges faced by the Sumerians, from environmental hardships to social strife, providing a framework to understand and overcome these difficulties. Through the stories of Enki's confrontations with his adversaries, the Mesopotamians explored themes of resilience, innovation, and the pursuit of balance, offering timeless lessons on the nature of conflict and the possibility of reconciliation.

Enki's adversaries, from rival gods to cosmic monsters, play a vital role in shaping the mythology of Mesopotamia, contributing to the rich tapestry of stories that define the civilization's spiritual landscape. These figures, often representing chaos, ignorance, or hubris, serve as foils to Enki's wisdom and creativity, highlighting his importance in the maintenance of order and the promotion of progress. The mythology surrounding these adversaries and their confrontations with Enki provides a narrative space in which the Sumerians could engage with the existential questions of their time, reflecting on the nature of evil, the challenges of leadership, and the enduring quest for harmony in a changing world. Enki's role as a deity of wisdom, innovation, and diplomacy is celebrated through these stories, affirming his status as a key figure in the Sumerian pantheon and a guardian of the cosmic order.

# RITUALS AND FESTIVALS

## ANNUAL CELEBRATIONS IN HONOR OF ENKI

The annual celebrations in honor of Enki encapsulate the deep reverence and affection the Sumerians held for this deity of wisdom, water, and life. These festivities, rich in symbolism and communal participation, were not merely observances of divine homage but profound expressions of gratitude and acknowledgment of Enki's role in sustaining civilization. Central to these celebrations were rituals that symbolized Enki's creative powers and contributions to the land's fertility and the people's well-being. The ceremonies blended music, prayer, and offerings, drawing the community together in a shared experience of worship and celebration. This communal aspect of the festivities highlights the Sumerians' belief in the gods' immanence in their daily lives, viewing these annual celebrations as vital links between the divine and the earthly realms.

The nature of these celebrations varied, with some focusing on the agricultural cycle, commemorating Enki's gift of fertile lands and abundant harvests. Others emphasized his role as the source of freshwater, vital for irrigation and sustenance. Through dances, processions, and the enactment of myths, the people reconnected with the sacred stories that framed their understanding of the world. These annual celebrations served as reminders of the covenant between Enki and humanity, a time for renewal of faith and reaffirming the community's place within the cosmic order. The participatory nature of these events, involving everyone from the highest priest to the ordinary farmer, underscored the universal impact of Enki's blessings, reinforcing social bonds and collective identity.

### RITES OF PASSAGE AND INITIATION

Rites of passage and initiation ceremonies were integral to Sumerian society, marking the transition of individuals through the stages of life and into the community's spiritual and social fabric. Enki, as a deity associated with wisdom and the mysteries of life, played a central role in these rites, which were often conducted within the precincts of his temples. These ceremonies were not mere formalities but deeply symbolic acts that connected the individual to the divine, the community, and the natural world. Through rituals that involved water, symbolic of purification and renewal, participants were reborn into new roles, whether it was transitioning from childhood to adulthood, entering the priesthood, or assuming a new social status. These rites of passage underscored the importance of the divine in guiding and protecting individuals throughout their lives, with

# ENKI AND THE WORLD ORDER

Enki's presence invoked to bestow wisdom and blessings upon the initiates.

The initiation ceremonies, particularly those related to the priesthood, were elaborate affairs that symbolized the acolyte's entry into a life of service to the gods and the community. These rites often included teachings on sacred texts, the secrets of the temple, and the rituals and incantations that facilitated communication with the divine. The role of Enki in these ceremonies highlighted his significance as a source of esoteric knowledge and divine wisdom, essential for the maintenance of order and the well-being of society. Through these rites of passage and initiation, individuals were woven into the broader tapestry of Sumerian religious and cultural life, ensuring the continuity of traditions and community cohesion.

## THE AKITU FESTIVAL

The Akitu Festival, which was celebrated at the beginning of the Babylonian New Year, was a significant event that transcended local deity worship to encompass the entire Mesopotamian pantheon, including Enki. Although primarily associated with Marduk in Babylon, the festival's themes of renewal, creation, and divine kingship resonated with Enki's role within the cosmic order. The Akitu Festival was a time when the gods were believed to renew their vows to humanity, reaffirming their commitment to uphold the cosmos's balance and ensure the earth's fertility. This celebration, lasting twelve days, involved a series of rituals that reenacted the creation of the world and the gods' victory over the forces of chaos, symbolizing the ongoing struggle to maintain order in the universe.

One of the festival's highlights was the procession of statues, where deities were symbolically brought together to participate in the sacred ceremonies, underscoring the unity of the divine realm and its relationship with the human world. This act of bringing the gods into the city and the temple served as a physical and spiritual renewal of their presence and power within the community. The Akitu Festival, with its rich tapestry of rituals and ceremonies, offered the people a direct engagement with the divine narrative, reinforcing the bonds between the gods and humanity and between the individuals and their community. It was a time of reflection, celebration, and hope, embodying the cycles of life, death, and rebirth that defined the Mesopotamian understanding of existence.

## WATER RITUALS AND PURIFICATION

In a civilization where water was both a life-giving resource and a symbol of purity, water rituals and purification ceremonies held a place of paramount importance. Enki, as the god of water, was intrinsically linked to these practices, with his temples often serving as centers for rituals that cleansed the body and the spirit. These ceremonies were not only acts of physical hygiene but deeply spiritual processes that prepared individuals for communion with the divine, removed impurities, and protected against malevolent forces. Water, in this context, was seen as a medium through which Enki's blessings flowed, offering renewal and sanctification. The act of purification extended beyond the individual to the community and the land, with rituals conducted to ensure the fertility of the fields and the clarity of the waterways, invoking Enki's power to nurture and protect.

# ENKI AND THE WORLD ORDER

The symbolic use of water in these rituals reflects the Sumerians' profound understanding of its dual nature—its capacity to both sustain life and cleanse it of impurity. Through the invocation of Enki in these ceremonies, water became a conduit for divine grace, imbuing it with the power to transform and renew. These practices illustrate the interconnectedness of the physical and spiritual worlds in Mesopotamian thought, where the mundane act of washing could have profound religious and cosmological implications. Water rituals and purification ceremonies, therefore, were essential components of Sumerian religious life, embodying the civilization's reverence for water and its custodian, Enki.

## MAGIC AND INCANTATIONS

Magic and incantations, integral to the Mesopotamian worldview, were mediums through which individuals could interact with the divine forces that permeated the cosmos. Enki, as the god of wisdom and the deep, was closely associated with the esoteric knowledge underpinning magical practices. Priests and practitioners sought Enki's favor and guidance in their magical workings, invoking his name in spells and rituals designed to heal, protect, and divine. These incantations were not mere words but potent expressions of will, believed to have the power to alter reality, to command spirits, and to invoke divine intervention. The use of magic and incantations highlights the Sumerians' belief in the accessibility of the divine and the potential for human agency to effect change within the cosmic order.

The practice of magic in Mesopotamia was a sophisticated art grounded in an intricate understanding of the natural world and its connection to the divine. With his dominion over the hidden depths and his mastery of secrets, Enki was the patron of this art, bestowing upon his followers the knowledge necessary to navigate the complexities of the spiritual realm. These practices underscore the Mesopotamians' nuanced view of power, where the ability to communicate with and influence the divine was mediated through ritual, symbol, and the spoken word. Magic and incantations, therefore, served as vital tools for coping with the uncertainties of life, embodying civilization's quest for knowledge, control, and harmony with the forces of the universe.

## PRIESTHOOD AND TEMPLE SERVICES

The priesthood played a crucial role in Mesopotamian society, acting as intermediaries between the divine and the mortal realms. Those who served in Enki's temples were not only caretakers of sacred spaces but also guardians of knowledge, responsible for the performance of rituals, the teaching of esoteric lore, and the maintenance of the cosmic order. The services performed by these priests were varied, encompassing offerings, sacrifices, divination, and the interpretation of dreams; each act was a reaffirmation of the community's bond with Enki. The dedication of these individuals to their god and their community illustrates the centrality of the temple in Sumerian life, serving as a hub of religious, social, and educational activity.

The temple services conducted in honor of Enki were elaborate affairs designed to ensure the god's favor and the continued prosperity of the city. Through daily rituals, annual festivals, and special ceremonies, the priests sought to align the will of the gods with that of the people, securing divine blessings and protection. The role of the priesthood in this process was indispensable, requiring a deep understanding of ritual practice, divine lore, and the needs of the community. Through their service, the priests of Enki bridged the gap between heaven and earth, playing a pivotal role in the sustenance of Mesopotamian civilization.

## THE LEGACY OF MESOPOTAMIAN RITUALS

The legacy of Mesopotamian rituals, embodied in the practices dedicated to Enki and the pantheon of gods, continues to influence our understanding of the ancient world. These rituals, with their rich symbolism and communal participation, offer insights into the Sumerians' conception of the divine, their relationship with the environment, and their views on society and governance. The enduring fascination with these ancient practices speaks to the universal human quest for connection with something greater than ourselves —a search for meaning in the cosmos. Through the study of Mesopotamian rituals, we gain a deeper appreciation for the complexity of this early civilization, its contributions to religious thought, and its impact on subsequent cultures.

The rituals and festivals dedicated to Enki and his fellow deities underscore the interconnectedness of religion, culture, and daily life in Mesopotamia. These practices were not only expressions of faith but also vital components of the social and political fabric, reinforcing bonds within the community and affirming the cosmic order. The legacy of these rituals, preserved through cuneiform texts and archaeological discoveries, continues to enchant and educate, providing a window into the spiritual life of one of humanity's earliest civilizations. Through the remnants of temples, the echoes of ancient hymns, and the mysteries of ritual practice, the spirit of Mesopotamia lives on, a testament to the enduring power of religious expression and human creativity.

# SYMBOLS AND ICONOGRAPHY

## THE GOAT-FISH AND CAPRICORN

The symbol of the Goat-Fish, deeply associated with Enki, is a fascinating amalgamation of terrestrial and aquatic elements, embodying the dual nature of this deity's dominion over both land and water. This composite creature, later associated with the zodiac sign Capricorn, encapsulates the essence of Enki's powers—fertility, creativity, and the fluidity of wisdom that transcends boundaries. The Goat-Fish's presence in Mesopotamian iconography is a testament to Enki's importance in the ancient world, symbolizing the interconnectedness of all life forms and the cyclical nature of existence. This icon not only represented Enki's role as a god of water and agriculture but also his ability to navigate the complexities of the cosmos, bridging the gap between the heavens and the earth.

The constellation of Capricorn carries on the Goat-Fish tradition in the stars by incorporating Enki's characteristics into the celestial tapestry that both ancient and contemporary civilizations have observed. The enduring nature of this symbol across cultures and epochs speaks to the universal appeal of its underlying themes—adaptation, resilience, and the union of opposites. The Goat-Fish, in its blending of the aquatic and the terrestrial, invites contemplation on the balance of nature and the harmonious coexistence of diverse elements, a concept as relevant today as it was in the time of Enki.

## THE CADUCEUS AND MODERN MEDICINE

The Caduceus, often associated with modern medicine, traces its origins to ancient Mesopotamian symbolism, where it was linked to Enki and his role as a healer and protector. This staff, which has serpents entwined around it and wings on top, represents the fusion of divine knowledge and the healing arts and reflects Enki's in-depth familiarity with both the natural and supernatural worlds. The use of the Caduceus in today's medical emblem underscores the lasting influence of ancient symbols on contemporary practices, serving as a bridge between the past and the present. It reminds us of the enduring quest for healing and understanding, principles that Enki championed through his teachings and interventions.

The transformation of the Caduceus from a symbol of divine protection to a representation of medical practice illustrates the fluidity of symbols across time and cultures. Its adoption by modern medicine is a testament to humanity's continuous reverence for the concepts of healing and renewal, values that Enki embodied. The Caduceus, in its modern context, continues to evoke a sense of balance and duality—between health and disease, science and spirituality—echoing Enki's mastery over life's complexities and the ancient belief in the gods' power to heal and protect.

## WATER AS A SYMBOL OF LIFE AND WISDOM

In Mesopotamia's cosmology, water was not merely a physical necessity but a profound symbol of life, wisdom, and creation, elements that Enki personified. As the god of the sweet waters, Enki's association with this life-giving element underscores the fundamental belief in water's sacred nature, its role as the source of all fertility, and the medium through which wisdom flows. This symbolism permeates Mesopotamian art and literature, where water is often depicted as a divine force capable of both nourishing the land and carrying the words of the gods. Enki's connection to water highlights his dual role as a creator and a communicator, bridging the divine and the mortal through the currents of knowledge and life.

The portrayal of water as a symbol of wisdom in Mesopotamian culture reflects the civilization's deep understanding of the natural world and its cycles. Through rituals, myths, and the veneration of deities like Enki, the Sumerians celebrated water's transformative power, recognizing its capacity to shape destinies and civilizations. This reverence for water, seen in the construction of canals, temples, and gardens, was an expression of gratitude and a recognition of humanity's place within a larger cosmic order. In the figure of Enki, water becomes a metaphor for the flow of time, the depth of knowledge, and the essence of life itself, embodying the interconnectedness of all things.

## ENKI'S THRONE AND THE ABZU

Enki's throne, situated within the Abzu, the primordial source of freshwater, symbolizes his authority over the depths and the mysteries they contain. This throne is not just a seat of power but a point of connection between the earthly and the divine, embodying Enki's role as the keeper of cosmic secrets and the patron of wisdom. The imagery surrounding Enki's throne, often depicted with motifs of flowing water and aquatic creatures, serves to reinforce his dominion over the life-giving waters and his role as a mediator between the known and the unknown. This iconography invites contemplation on the nature of wisdom and power, suggesting that true authority stems from an understanding of the fundamental forces that govern life.

The Abzu, as Enki's domain, represents the untapped potential and the raw materials from which creation springs. The throne within this sacred space symbolizes the god's ability to harness these chaotic forces, shaping them into the order that sustains the universe. This imagery emphasizes the Mesopotamians' conception of the cosmos as a place of dynamic balance where chaos and order are constantly interacting through the wisdom of deities like Enki. The throne in the Abzu, therefore, is more than an artifact of divine rule; it is a symbol of the creative potential that lies in understanding and mastering the mysteries of existence.

## SACRED NUMBERS AND GEOMETRY

The Mesopotamians attributed profound significance to numbers and geometric patterns, viewing them as sacred codes that underpin the structure of the cosmos. Enki, as a god of wisdom and creation, is closely associated with this numerical and geometric symbolism, which is evident in the design of temples, the layout of cities, and the structure of rituals. These patterns were not merely aesthetic choices but reflections of a deeper cosmological understanding, embodying the harmony and order that Enki and his fellow deities sought to instill in the world. The use of sacred numbers and geometry in Mesopotamian culture demonstrates that the civilization believed in a universe with discernible laws, with mathematics serving as a language that could comprehend and replicate the divine order.

Incorporating these principles into religious and civic architecture was an act of homage to the gods, an attempt to mirror the perfection of the celestial realm on Earth. Temples constructed with these sacred proportions were seen as physical manifestations of the cosmic order, spaces where the divine and the human could interact. Through the use of sacred numbers and geometry, the Sumerians expressed their understanding of the universe as an intricately designed system, with Enki as one of its master architects. This symbolism, woven into the fabric of their civilization, serves as a reminder of the profound connection between the material and the spiritual, the earthly and the divine.

## THE ROLE OF ARTIFACTS IN WORSHIP

Artifacts played a crucial role in Mesopotamian worship practices, serving as conduits for divine presence and aiding in the performance of rituals. These objects, ranging from statues and votive offerings to ritual instruments and temple furnishings, were imbued with symbolic meaning, representing the gods' attributes and stories. Enki's worship, in particular, utilized artifacts that symbolized his dominion over water, wisdom, and creation, such as vessels for libations, models of the Abzu, and representations of the Goat-Fish. These items were not merely decorative but were integral to the enactment of rituals, facilitating communication with the divine and the manifestation of Enki's blessings.

The use of artifacts in worship allowed for a tangible connection to the divine, enabling worshippers to express their devotion, seek guidance, and participate in the sacred narratives that defined their relationship with the gods. Through the offering of votive gifts, the recreation of mythological scenes, and the use of ritual instruments, the faithful engaged with the divine on a personal and communal level, reinforcing the bonds between the gods and humanity. The role of artifacts in Mesopotamian worship practices underscores the material culture's importance in religious expression, revealing the depth of the civilization's spiritual life and the centrality of deities like Enki in the people's everyday experiences.

## INTERPRETING ANCIENT ART

The interpretation of ancient Mesopotamian art offers invaluable insights into the civilization's religious beliefs, social structures, and cosmological understanding. Scholars and enthusiasts alike can unravel the layers of meaning embedded in these ancient works by studying the symbols, iconography, and artifacts associated with Enki and the broader pantheon. The depiction of gods, the use of sacred numbers and patterns, and the representation of mythological narratives in art provide a window into the

Mesopotamians' worldview, illuminating their perceptions of the divine, the natural world, and the place of humans within the cosmos.

This interpretive endeavor is not merely an academic exercise but a bridge that connects us to our shared human past, allowing us to engage with the thoughts, fears, and aspirations of those who lived thousands of years ago. The art of ancient Mesopotamia, with its rich symbolism and intricate detail, invites us to ponder the mysteries of existence and the search for meaning that has defined the human experience across millennia. Through the careful study of these artifacts, we continue the conversation with our ancestors, exploring the depths of wisdom and creativity that characterized one of humanity's earliest civilizations.

# ENKI IN LITERATURE

## THE EPIC OF GILGAMESH

In "The Epic of Gilgamesh," one of the most venerable pieces of literature from ancient Mesopotamia, the presence and influence of Enki, although not always direct, permeate through the themes of wisdom, creation, and the quest for immortality. Enki's embodiment of knowledge and the cyclical nature of life provides a backdrop to Gilgamesh's journey, offering a silent yet profound commentary on the pursuits that define humanity. While Enki himself may not stand at the forefront of the epic's narrative, his essence is interwoven with the quest of Gilgamesh, reflecting the god's role in guiding and shaping the destinies of men and gods alike. The epic serves not just as a tale of adventure but as a meditation on the limits of human ambition and the wisdom required to accept the fundamental truths of existence, themes deeply associated with Enki's domain.

Gilgamesh's encounters with characters like Utnapishtim, the survivor of the Mesopotamian flood, further echo Enki's teachings and interventions, illustrating the interconnectedness of divine wisdom and human endeavor. This narrative convergence highlights Enki's significance in Mesopotamian thought as a deity who not only crafts the world but also imparts the knowledge necessary for understanding the value of life and the inevitability of death. The epic, in its exploration of friendship, loss, and the search for meaning, encapsulates the complexities of the human condition, offering insights that remain relevant in the modern world. Through its portrayal of Gilgamesh's trials and revelations, the epic underscores the enduring relevance of Enki's wisdom, emphasizing the importance of balance, compassion, and acceptance in the face of life's impermanence.

## ENKI AND THE WORLD ORDER

"Enki and the World Order," a myth that delves into the god's endeavors to organize the universe and establish civilization, stands as a testament to Enki's prowess and foresight. This narrative not only showcases Enki's role as a creator and sustainer but also highlights his diplomatic skills in dealing with both gods and humans. The text outlines the vast array of responsibilities Enki assumes, from the allocation of resources to the institution of societal norms, underscoring God's integral role in the maintenance of cosmic and social harmony. This literature piece illuminates the Sumerians' view of the universe as a well-ordered system where balance is achieved through the careful administration of the divine.

Within this story, Enki's interactions with other deities and his solutions to the challenges that arise in the establishment of the world order exemplify his wisdom and creativity. The narrative serves as an allegory for the principles that underpin Mesopotamian society, reflecting the belief in a structured cosmos where each element, whether divine or mortal, has its place and purpose. "Enki and the World Order" not only entertains but also educates, offering a glimpse into the values and ideologies that shaped ancient Mesopotamian culture. Through the figure of Enki, the myth articulates a vision of leadership and responsibility that resonates with timeless questions about power, stewardship, and the ethics of governance.

## THE DESCENT OF INANNA

"The Descent of Inanna" is a profound narrative that explores themes of death, rebirth, and transformation, with Enki playing a crucial role in the goddess's journey into the underworld and her subsequent return. In this myth, Inanna's descent represents a metaphorical exploration of the cycles of life and the necessity of facing the darkness to emerge renewed. Enki's intervention on behalf of Inanna, through the creation of beings to rescue her, symbolizes the god's understanding of the need for balance between the forces of life and death and his compassion in the face of suffering. This story highlights Enki's attributes as a deity capable of empathy and innovation, using his knowledge to restore order and ensure the continuity of life.

The narrative underscores the interconnectedness of all realms of existence, from the heavens to the underworld, and the role of the gods in mediating these transitions. Enki's wisdom and ingenuity in assisting Inanna's return illuminate the Mesopotamian belief in the possibility of redemption and renewal, even in the face of seemingly insurmountable odds. "The Descent of Inanna" is a powerful testament to the themes of sacrifice, resilience, and the transformative power of love and wisdom—qualities Enki embodies. Through this myth, the ancient Mesopotamians conveyed their understanding of the complexities of the divine and human experiences, offering insights into the eternal cycle of death and rebirth that defines the cosmos.

## LAMENTATIONS AND PRAYERS

Lamentations and prayers form a significant part of Mesopotamian literature, expressing the depths of human emotion and the emotional appeal to the divine for guidance, protection, and relief from suffering. In these texts, Enki is often invoked as a source of solace and wisdom, a deity whose understanding and benevolence can alleviate the hardships of the mortal condition. These writings not only reflect the personal and communal struggles of the ancient Mesopotamians but also highlight their profound relationship with the gods, particularly with Enki, whose attributes of compassion and insight are sought in times of distress. The lamentations and prayers articulate a complex theology where divine intervention is intertwined with human agency, illustrating the Sumerians' nuanced approach to fate, free will, and the power of supplication.

The recitation of these texts, whether in the quiet of a temple or the expanse of a public gathering, served as a cathartic expression of faith and a reaffirmation of the community's bond with the divine. Through these lamentations and prayers, the ancient Mesopotamians navigated the uncertainties of life, drawing on Enki's wisdom and mercy to find strength and hope. These literary pieces, rich in imagery and emotion, provide a window into the spiritual life of Mesopotamia, revealing the depth of their engagement with the divine and the resilience of their spirit in the face of adversity. Enki, as a deity intimately connected with the human experience, occupies a central place in these expressions of longing and devotion, embodying the ancient Mesopotamians' quest for understanding and redemption.

## WISDOM LITERATURE AND PROVERBS

Wisdom literature and proverbs in ancient Mesopotamia served as vehicles for the transmission of moral and philosophical teachings, embodying the collective knowledge and ethical considerations of society. Enki, as the god of wisdom and cunning intelligence, is a figure that looms large in this literary tradition, often depicted as the ultimate source of the insights and guidelines that inform human conduct. These texts, ranging from instructions for living a virtuous life to reflections on the nature of justice and power, draw upon Enki's archetype as the sage deity, offering practical and spiritual advice that resonates with the challenges of human existence. The wisdom literature and proverbs underscore the importance of knowledge, prudence, and ethical behavior, reflecting the Sumerians' belief in the value of learning and the cultivation of virtue.

The teachings encapsulated in these literary works are not merely didactic but are imbued with a deep understanding of the complexities of life and the human condition. Through the figure of Enki, these texts advocate for a balanced approach to life, emphasizing the need for harmony between the individual, society, and the divine. The wisdom literature and proverbs of Mesopotamia, with their emphasis on moral integrity, social responsibility, and the pursuit of knowledge, serve as a testament to the civilization's intellectual and spiritual achievements. Through these writings, Enki's influence extends beyond the mythological and into the realms of everyday life, guiding individuals in their quest for wisdom and ethical living.

## ENKI'S INFLUENCE ON LATER TEXTS

Enki's influence on later texts and traditions is a testament to the enduring legacy of this deity in the tapestry of human culture and religious thought. His characteristics of wisdom, creativity, and protective benevolence have found echoes in subsequent mythologies and philosophical systems, illustrating the broad impact of Mesopotamian beliefs on the development of cultural and religious ideas. The motifs and themes associated with Enki, from the creation of humanity to the navigation of life's moral and existential dilemmas, have permeated various literary and religious traditions, adapting to new contexts while retaining the essence of the original myths. This cross-cultural resonance highlights the universal themes embodied by Enki, such as the quest for knowledge, the value of compassion, and the importance of harmony between opposing forces.

The adaptation and reinterpretation of Enki's myths in later texts underscore the fluidity of mythological narratives and their capacity to inspire and inform across generations and cultures. Enki's role as a teacher and guide resonates with the human desire for understanding and connection, making his stories relevant to diverse audiences seeking wisdom in the face of life's challenges. Through the continued study and appreciation of these ancient texts, Enki's legacy as a deity of profound insight and benevolence continues to inspire contemporary explorations of spirituality, ethics, and the human condition. The enduring influence of Enki on later texts and traditions is a reflection of the deep impact of Mesopotamian culture on the collective human heritage, underscoring the timeless relevance of its wisdom and mythology.

## COMPARATIVE ANALYSIS OF MYTHOLOGICAL THEMES

A comparative analysis of mythological themes across different cultures reveals the universal aspects of human storytelling and the shared concerns that have occupied societies throughout history. Enki, with his complex role as creator, protector, and trickster, embodies themes that resonate across mythological traditions, such as the tension between order and chaos, the quest for knowledge, and the dynamics of power and responsibility. By examining Enki's narratives alongside those of other deities from various cultures, we uncover the common threads that weave through humanity's mythological tapestry, highlighting our collective fascination with creation, wisdom, and the moral ambiguities of existence. This cross-cultural exploration enriches our understanding of Enki and his place within the broader context of world mythology, offering insights into the similarities and differences that define our spiritual and philosophical inquiries.

The themes associated with Enki—his engagement with the natural world, his interventions in human affairs, and his embodiment of wisdom and duality—reflect the universal questions and challenges that have shaped human consciousness. Through a comparative analysis, we appreciate the nuances of Enki's character and his relevance to contemporary discussions about ethics, leadership, and the human relationship with the environment. The study of Enki and his counterparts in other mythological systems underscores the enduring power of myth to articulate the depths of the human experience, providing a rich source of reflection and inspiration for navigating the complexities of life. In the figure of Enki, we find a mirror of our own struggles and aspirations, a deity whose stories continue to resonate with the timeless quest for understanding, balance, and connection in an ever-changing world.

# COMPARATIVE MYTHOLOGY

## ENKI AND EGYPTIAN GODS

The comparison between Enki and Egyptian deities unveils a fascinating tapestry of cross-cultural mythological themes, particularly with gods such as Thoth and Osiris. Like Enki, Thoth is a deity of wisdom, credited with the invention of writing and regarded as the mediator between conflicting forces, underscoring the universal valorization of knowledge and communication across ancient civilizations. Similarly, Osiris's association with the Nile's life-giving floods and the cyclical nature of agriculture mirror Enki's connection to water and fertility, highlighting the foundational role of water deities in sustaining life and civilization. These parallels not only illuminate the shared human experience of seeking to understand and personify the natural world but also reflect the complex ways in which cultures perceive the divine's role in creation, knowledge, and the afterlife.

The interactions between Enki and the Egyptian gods, though fictional in a direct sense, reveal the underlying commonalities in how ancient peoples conceptualized their relationship with the divine and the environment. The narrative of Enki navigating the waters of the Abzu resonates with the story of Osiris navigating the underworld, both embodying the themes of death, rebirth, and the perpetual cycle of life. This comparison extends beyond mere thematic similarities, delving into the core of ancient religious thought, where gods serve as embodiments of natural forces and human ideals, guiding and shaping the moral and material world.

## SIMILARITIES WITH GREEK MYTHOLOGY

Exploring the similarities between Enki and figures from Greek mythology, such as Prometheus and Poseidon, offers a window into the shared mythological structures that underpin diverse cultures. Prometheus, the bringer of fire and the benefactor of humanity, shares Enki's trickster qualities and his defiance against higher authorities to aid mankind, illustrating the archetype of the cultural hero who risks divine wrath to empower humanity. Poseidon's dominion over the seas and his role in earthquakes and storms echo Enki's control over water and his capacity to both nurture and destroy, highlighting the universal depiction of water deities as powerful and ambivalent figures within human societies.

These analogies are not merely coincidental but speak to the deep psychological and environmental influences that shape human storytelling and religious belief. The narratives of Enki, Prometheus, and Poseidon reflect a collective attempt to make sense of the natural world's capriciousness, attributing its unpredictability to the whims of powerful deities. Through these stories, ancient peoples communicated their understanding of humanity's place within the cosmos, grappling with themes of creation, innovation, and the fraught relationship between the divine and the mortal realm.

## PARALLELS IN HINDU AND BUDDHIST TRADITIONS

The examination of Enki within the context of Hindu and Buddhist traditions reveals intriguing parallels, particularly with deities such as Varuna and Avalokiteshvara. Varuna, the Vedic god of water and the celestial ocean, shares similarities with Enki in his governance over the waters and his role as a keeper of cosmic order and law, emphasizing the cross-cultural significance of water as a symbol of life and moral authority. Avalokiteshvara, the bodhisattva of compassion, reflects aspects of Enki's benevolence and wisdom, embodying the principle of empathy and assistance to all beings, a testament to the universal human values of kindness and understanding.

These parallels extend beyond the superficial comparisons of domain and attribute, touching upon the deeper, shared human concerns with justice, compassion, and the stewardship of the natural world. The stories of Varuna and Avalokiteshvara, like those of Enki, serve as cultural expressions of the desire for balance, harmony, and the alleviation of suffering, showcasing the profound connections that bind diverse religious traditions. Through the lens of comparative mythology, we observe not only the unique characteristics of each deity but also the common threads that weave through humanity's spiritual heritage, highlighting the collective quest for understanding and the articulation of universal truths through the mythic narrative.

## THE ARCHETYPE OF THE TRICKSTER

Enki, the archetype of the trickster in Mesopotamian mythology, has counterparts in many different cultures, demonstrating the trickster's function as a universal symbol of change, creativity, and the disruption of order. Figures such as Loki in Norse mythology and Coyote in Native American tales share Enki's penchant for mischief and his ability to navigate and sometimes subvert established norms for higher purposes or personal gain. These characters play crucial roles in their respective mythologies, challenging the status quo and introducing elements of unpredictability and innovation, reflecting the human fascination with the boundaries of morality, the limits of power, and the potential for transformation.

The trickster's appeal lies in its embodiment of the complexity of human nature, representing the dual capacity for creation and destruction, wisdom and folly. Through the exploits of trickster figures, cultures express their understanding of the world as a place of inherent contradictions, where chaos and order are in constant flux. The trickster's actions, often motivated by a combination of altruism and self-interest, invite reflection on the nature of wisdom, the consequences of curiosity, and the inevitable interplay between the divine and the mundane. Enki, with his clever interventions and creative solutions, exemplifies the trickster's role as an agent of change, challenging both gods and humans to adapt, evolve, and reconsider their place within the cosmos.

## WATER DEITIES ACROSS CULTURES

Enki serves as an example of the water deity motif, which appears frequently in world mythologies to represent the fundamental role that water plays in sustaining life and forming human consciousness. Deities such as Yemoja in Yoruba religion, Tlaloc in Aztec mythology, and Danu in Celtic beliefs all personify water's life-giving and destructive aspects, embodying the dual nature of this essential element. These deities, like Enki, are revered for their ability to bestow fertility, purify and heal, and wield water's transformative power, reflecting the universal human reverence for water as a source of life, renewal, and spiritual cleansing.

The widespread veneration of water deities underscores the shared recognition of water's critical importance in agricultural, societal, and spiritual realms, highlighting the deep connection between human communities and their natural environments. Through the worship and mythologizing of water deities, cultures articulate their understanding of the natural world's cycles, the necessity of balance, and the respect and stewardship required to maintain harmony with this vital resource. Enki's representation within this pantheon of water gods serves as a reminder of the commonalities that bind diverse cultures together, celebrating water's role as a source of life, wisdom, and inspiration across the ages.

## ENKI AND THE GLOBAL FLOOD MYTHS

The narrative of the global flood, prominently featured in the story of Enki, is a motif that transcends cultural boundaries, appearing in various forms, from the biblical account of Noah to the Hindu story of Manu. These flood myths, while differing in details, share core themes of divine retribution, human survival, and the renewal of life, reflecting widespread human concerns with morality, destruction, and rebirth. Enki's role in warning Utnapishtim of the impending deluge and providing the means for survival mirrors the actions of deities and heroes in other traditions, who act as intermediaries between the divine will and the fate of humanity.

The ubiquity of flood myths suggests a collective attempt to make sense of natural disasters and their impact on human societies, framing them within narratives of divine judgment and redemption. These stories serve as cautionary tales and lessons in humility, resilience, and the importance of maintaining a harmonious relationship with the divine and the natural world. Enki's intervention in the Mesopotamian flood myth highlights his character as a protector of humanity and a proponent of renewal, embodying the hope that even in the face of overwhelming catastrophe, there exists the possibility for a new beginning and the continuation of life.

## SYNCRETISM AND CULTURAL EXCHANGE

The phenomenon of syncretism, where religious beliefs and practices merge and influence one another, is evident in the spread and adaptation of Enki's mythology across cultures and epochs. This blending of traditions reflects the dynamic nature of religious thought and the interconnectedness of human societies, with deities like Enki acquiring new attributes and associations as their stories are told and retold in different contexts. Trade, conquest, and migration facilitate the process of cultural exchange, which enriches the tapestry of world mythology by fostering the exchange of ideas and the emergence of fresh modes of spiritual expression.

Syncretism highlights the adaptability of mythological themes and the universality of certain archetypes, underscoring the shared human endeavor to understand the divine and articulate the mysteries of existence. Through the lens of syncretism, Enki's mythology can be seen as part of a broader dialogue between cultures, contributing to a collective heritage of myth and legend. This exchange of beliefs and narratives fosters a deeper appreciation for the diversity of human spirituality and the common threads that weave through the world's religious traditions, celebrating the richness of our shared mythological heritage and the enduring legacy of figures like Enki in the quest for meaning and connection in an ever-changing world.

# ENKI'S LEGACY IN MODERN CULTURE

## ENKI IN NEW AGE BELIEFS

Enki has found a resurgence in New Age beliefs, where his ancient wisdom and association with water, fertility, and creation resonate with contemporary spiritual seekers. In this modern context, Enki is often seen as a symbol of the interconnectedness of all life and a guardian of hidden knowledge and esoteric truths. Followers of New Age spirituality draw upon Enki's mythology to explore themes of personal transformation, healing, and harmony with the natural world, viewing him as a guide in the quest for enlightenment and self-discovery. This adaptation of Enki's attributes reflects a broader trend in New Age thought, where ancient deities are reinterpreted to address the spiritual and existential questions of the modern era, emphasizing the timeless relevance of these mythological figures.

The integration of Enki into New Age practices showcases the fluidity of myth and its capacity to evolve and find new expressions in different cultural and temporal contexts. Through meditation, ritual, and the study of ancient texts, adherents seek to connect with Enki's wisdom, applying his teachings to contemporary life challenges. This revival of interest in Enki and other ancient deities highlights a growing desire for a deeper understanding of the human condition and a more profound connection with the cosmos, demonstrating the enduring appeal of mythological narratives in providing insight and inspiration.

## THE GOD IN SCIENCE FICTION AND FANTASY

Enki's legacy extends into the realms of science fiction and fantasy, where his characteristics as a creator, trickster, and master of waters inspire characters, plots, and settings. Authors and creators in these genres often draw upon Enki's mythology to craft stories that explore themes of creation, technology, and the ethical dilemmas associated with power and knowledge. In these narratives, Enki-like figures appear as ancient aliens, powerful wizards, or wise mentors, guiding protagonists through complex worlds where the boundaries between the natural and the supernatural blur. This fusion of ancient myth with speculative fiction opens new avenues for examining contemporary issues, such as the impact of technology on society, environmental degradation, and the quest for meaning in an increasingly complex world.

The portrayal of Enki in science fiction and fantasy not only entertains but also invites reflection on the nature of creativity, the responsibilities of creators, and the potential for both benevolence and mischief in the exercise of power. These stories, by reimagining Enki's mythology in futuristic or alternate universes, underscore the versatility of myth in providing a framework for grappling with eternal human concerns. The presence of Enki in these genres demonstrates the capacity of ancient myths to adapt and remain relevant, inspiring new generations of writers and readers to explore the depths of human imagination and the possibilities of the unknown.

## ENKI IN POPULAR LITERATURE

In popular literature, Enki emerges as a multifaceted character whose ancient tales are reinterpreted to resonate with contemporary audiences. Novels, poetry, and non-fiction works delve into Enki's mythology, exploring his role as a deity of wisdom, creation, and rebellion against the divine order. Through these literary explorations, Enki is cast in roles that reflect modern values and concerns, from environmental stewardship to the pursuit of knowledge and the challenge of authority. This reimagining of Enki's character and stories in popular literature serves not only to entertain but also to provoke thought on the relevance of ancient myths in addressing the complexities of modern life.

Authors draw upon Enki's rich narrative heritage to weave tales that span genres, from historical fiction and fantasy to philosophical treatises. These works invite readers to reconsider the significance of myth in contemporary society, offering insights into the human psyche, ethical dilemmas, and our relationship with the natural world. The adaptation of Enki's mythology in popular literature underscores the enduring power of storytelling in exploring and expressing the multifaceted nature of human experience. Enki's legacy continues to inspire, challenge, and entertain through these creative reinterpretations, bridging the gap between the ancient and the modern, the sacred and the secular.

## SYMBOLISM IN CONTEMPORARY ART

Contemporary artists frequently incorporate symbols associated with Enki into their work, exploring themes of creation, wisdom, and the fluidity of identity. Enki's connection to water and the primordial chaos serves as a potent metaphor for the creative process, inviting viewers to contemplate the origins of life and the interplay between order and disorder. Through various mediums, from sculpture and painting to digital installations, artists reinterpret Enki's mythology to comment on current issues, such as environmental degradation, technological advancement, and the search for meaning in an ever-changing world. This engagement with Enki's symbolism in contemporary art demonstrates the capacity of ancient myths to inspire and inform artistic expression, providing a rich source of imagery and ideas that resonate with modern sensibilities.

The depiction of Enki in art often challenges conventional narratives, presenting the deity in ways that blur the boundaries between the past and the present, the divine and the human. These artistic interpretations invite reflection on the continuity of human concerns across time and the potential for ancient wisdom to shed light on contemporary dilemmas. By drawing on Enki's mythology, contemporary artists engage in a dialogue with the past, exploring the ways in which these age-old stories can illuminate the complexities of modern existence and the enduring quest for understanding and connection.

## ENVIRONMENTALISM AND ENKI

Enki's association with water and fertility positions him as a symbolic figure in contemporary environmental movements, symbolizing the critical importance of preserving natural resources and maintaining ecological balance. Activists and environmentalists draw upon Enki's mythology to highlight the interconnectedness of all life and the necessity of stewarding the earth's waters with care and respect. In this context, Enki becomes a symbol of the potential for regeneration and sustainability, reminding us of the ancient wisdom that recognizes the earth as a living system deserving of protection and reverence. This application of Enki's legacy to environmentalism underscores the relevance of mythological narratives in framing our understanding of the natural world and our responsibilities within it.

The use of Enki's imagery in environmental advocacy serves to inspire a deeper appreciation for the planet's water systems as sources of life and sustenance, echoing the Sumerians' reverence for these essential elements. By invoking Enki's name and attributes, environmentalists connect contemporary concerns with the timeless recognition of water's sacredness, fostering a sense of continuity and urgency in the efforts to address ecological challenges. Enki's enduring presence in the environmental discourse exemplifies the power of myth to mobilize action, evoke empathy, and articulate a vision of harmony between humanity and the natural world, encouraging a collective commitment to ecological stewardship and sustainability.

## DIGITAL MEDIA AND VIDEO GAMES

Enki's legacy is reimagined and revitalized in digital media and video games, introducing the ancient deity to new audiences through interactive storytelling and immersive experiences. Enki appears as a character in various forms, from wise mentor and cryptic antagonist to a guide through worlds rich in mythological lore. These digital renditions of Enki's mythology offer players the opportunity to engage with ancient narratives in a contemporary medium, exploring themes of creation, knowledge, and the consequences of divine power within virtual environments. This integration of Enki into digital media underscores the adaptability of myth to new forms of cultural expression, demonstrating the ongoing fascination with ancient stories and their potential to enrich modern entertainment and educational content.

Video games, in particular, provide a unique platform for the exploration of Enki's character and mythology, allowing players to interact directly with the narratives and themes associated with the deity. Through quests, puzzles, and narrative choices, players navigate stories that draw on Enki's wisdom, creativity, and occasional trickery, experiencing firsthand the challenges and rewards of wielding divine powers. This medium's ability to breathe new life into ancient myths highlights the dynamic relationship between culture and technology, revealing the enduring appeal of figures like Enki in shaping our understanding of the past and its influence on contemporary imagination and creativity.

## THE RELEVANCE OF ANCIENT MYTHS TODAY

The enduring relevance of ancient myths, exemplified by the stories of Enki, lies in their capacity to articulate fundamental aspects of the human condition—our fears, aspirations, and the quest for understanding in a complex and often bewildering world. These myths, passed down through generations, continue to resonate because they address timeless questions about creation, morality, and the role of the divine in human affairs. In the modern era, where rapid technological advancements and societal changes pose new challenges, the ancient narratives of Enki and his contemporaries offer valuable insights into the enduring nature of these existential dilemmas and the potential for wisdom and compassion to guide human actions.

The continued fascination with Enki's mythology across various platforms—from literature and art to environmental advocacy and digital media—demonstrates the malleability of myth and its ability to adapt to changing cultural landscapes. By engaging with these ancient stories, contemporary society can find inspiration and guidance for navigating the complexities of the modern world, drawing on the rich well of human experience encapsulated in myth. Enki's legacy, with its emphasis on creativity, knowledge, and the balancing of opposing forces, serves as a reminder of the power of storytelling to connect us to our past, inform our present, and shape our understanding of what it means to be human in an ever-evolving universe. Through the continued exploration and reinterpretation of ancient myths, we affirm the value of these narratives in providing depth, context, and perspective to our collective journey.

# THE FUTURE OF ENKI STUDIES

## ARCHAEOLOGICAL PROSPECTS

The future of Enki studies holds great promise, mainly through the lens of archaeology, where untapped sites and emerging technologies offer new pathways to understanding this ancient deity's role and significance. As excavations continue in regions once part of the Sumerian empire, the potential to uncover artifacts, temples, and texts directly related to Enki could provide unparalleled insights into his worship, mythology, and influence on ancient Mesopotamian society. Each discovery has the potential to reshape our understanding of Enki, offering fresh perspectives on his attributes, the rituals dedicated to him, and his interactions with other deities and humanity. We will be able to understand Enki's position in the pantheon and his enduring legacy over millennia thanks to the dynamic nature of archaeological exploration and advancements in dating methods and site analysis.

The integration of new archaeological methodologies, such as remote sensing and non-invasive survey techniques, allows researchers to explore ancient sites with minimal disruption, preserving their integrity while revealing secrets buried for centuries. These technological advancements not only expand the scope of archaeological inquiry but also enhance the precision and reliability of findings, bringing us closer to the world Enki inhabited. As future excavations proceed, the collaborative efforts of archaeologists, historians, and scholars across disciplines are essential in piecing together the complex mosaic of Enki's mythology and its impact on the development of civilization. This interdisciplinary approach, rooted in both respect for the past and enthusiasm for the future, sets the stage for groundbreaking discoveries that will enrich our collective understanding of ancient Mesopotamia and its gods.

## TECHNOLOGICAL ADVANCES IN RESEARCH

Technological advancements in research are revolutionizing the study of Enki and Mesopotamian mythology by enabling academics to examine ancient texts and artifacts in unprecedented depth and clarity. Digital imaging and 3D reconstruction techniques allow for the virtual restoration of tablets, seals, and statues, offering new insights into the iconography and inscriptions associated with Enki. This digitization of ancient relics not only preserves them for future generations but also democratizes access to these materials, enabling researchers worldwide to examine and interpret them in innovative ways. Furthermore, computational linguistics and machine learning are transforming our ability to translate and understand cuneiform script, opening up vast archives of Mesopotamian literature to detailed analysis and interpretation.

These technological tools are not merely adjuncts to traditional research methods but are reshaping the landscape of Enki studies, fostering a more collaborative and interdisciplinary approach to ancient history and religion. By leveraging big data analytics, scholars can uncover patterns and connections within and across ancient texts, revealing new dimensions of Enki's character, his relationships with other deities, and his influence on human society. This integration of technology into the humanities enriches our grasp of ancient cultures, bridging the gap between the past and present and inviting a broader audience to engage with the complexities of Mesopotamian mythology.

## COMPARATIVE RELIGION AND MYTHOLOGY

The field of comparative religion and mythology offers fertile ground for the future exploration of Enki's legacy, providing a framework for understanding his role within a broader context of global mythological traditions. By examining Enki alongside deities from other ancient cultures, scholars can uncover universal themes and archetypes that transcend cultural and temporal boundaries, illuminating the shared human experience of the divine. This comparative approach enriches our comprehension of Enki, highlighting his uniqueness while situating him within the collective tapestry of world mythology. Such studies not only contribute to the academic understanding of ancient religions but also foster a deeper appreciation for the diversity and commonality of human belief systems across history.

Engaging with Enki through the lens of comparative religion and mythology encourages dialogue between traditions, promoting a multicultural appreciation of the ways in which different societies have grappled with questions of creation, wisdom, and the natural world. This cross-cultural exploration can reveal the adaptability of mythological motifs and their relevance to contemporary issues, such as environmental stewardship, ethical leadership, and the pursuit of knowledge. As scholars continue to draw connections between Enki and figures from other traditions, they pave the way for a more inclusive and nuanced understanding of mythology as a mirror of humanity's relationship with the cosmos, offering insights that resonate with the challenges and aspirations of the 21st century.

## THE ROLE OF DIGITAL HUMANITIES

The role of digital humanities in the study of Enki and Mesopotamian mythology represents a significant shift towards a more accessible and interactive approach to ancient studies. Digital archives, virtual reality simulations, and online platforms are transforming how we engage with the ancient world, allowing for immersive experiences that bring Enki's stories and the Sumerian civilization to life for a global audience. These digital tools not only facilitate scholarly research but also democratize access to knowledge, enabling educators, students, and the general public to explore the depths of Mesopotamian culture and religion from anywhere in the world. The integration of digital humanities into Enki studies encourages a participatory culture of learning where ancient texts and artifacts can be explored in virtual environments, fostering a deeper connection and understanding of this ancient deity's enduring legacy.

The potential for digital humanities to revolutionize the study of Enki extends beyond academic research, offering creative avenues for storytelling, gaming, and artistic expression inspired by Mesopotamian mythology. Interactive platforms can simulate ancient rituals, reconstruct temples dedicated to Enki, and visualize the cosmological landscapes of the Sumerian world, providing immersive educational experiences that engage the senses and the imagination. As digital humanities continue to evolve, the possibilities for exploring and disseminating the rich tapestry of Enki's mythology are boundless, promising to inspire new generations of scholars, creatives, and enthusiasts drawn to the ancient mysteries of Mesopotamia.

## REASSESSING ANCIENT TEXTS

The future of Enki studies also lies in the reassessment of ancient texts, where new interpretations and methodologies can yield fresh insights into the deity's complexities and nuances. Advances in decipherment techniques, coupled with a more critical approach to source material, promise to deepen our understanding of Enki's character, his interactions with other deities, and his influence on human affairs. This reevaluation of ancient texts, taking into account the socio-political and environmental contexts in which they were produced, allows for a more nuanced comprehension of Enki's role within Sumerian religion and mythology. As scholars revisit these texts with fresh eyes, the narratives of Enki are enriched, revealing layers of meaning that speak to the enduring relevance of ancient wisdom in addressing contemporary questions.

The interdisciplinary nature of modern research, incorporating insights from anthropology, psychology, and environmental studies, enhances the analysis of ancient texts, offering broader perspectives on Enki's significance. This holistic approach not only illuminates the multifaceted character of Enki but also encourages a deeper exploration of the values, beliefs, and practices of the Sumerian people. As we continue to reassess ancient texts, the stories of Enki emerge as vital sources of knowledge, reflecting the complexity of the human-divine relationship and the timeless quest for understanding the mysteries of existence.

## CULTURAL AND SPIRITUAL REVIVAL

In the 21st century and beyond, Enki's legacy is experiencing a cultural and spiritual revival as individuals and communities draw upon ancient myths to navigate the complexities of modern life. In an era of rapid technological change and environmental challenges, this resurgence of interest in Enki is a reflection of a broader search for meaning, connection, and sustainability. Through the revival of Enki's mythology, contemporary society can explore themes of creation, wisdom, and balance, finding inspiration in the ancient narratives to address today's concerns. This re-engagement with Enki's stories is not merely nostalgic but represents a conscious effort to reclaim and reinterpret ancient wisdom for the purpose of crafting a more harmonious and sustainable future.

The cultural and spiritual revival of Enki's mythology encourages a reexamination of our relationship with the natural world, urging a return to principles of stewardship and respect that are deeply embedded in ancient religious traditions. Enki, as a deity associated with water, fertility, and knowledge, serves as a powerful symbol for the integration of ecological awareness and spiritual depth in addressing contemporary environmental crises. As we look to Enki and the ancient myths for guidance, the potential for a cultural and spiritual renaissance grounded in the wisdom of the past offers hope and direction for navigating the challenges of the 21st century and beyond, underscoring the timeless relevance of ancient narratives in inspiring change and fostering a deeper understanding of our place within the cosmos.

## ENKI IN THE 21ST CENTURY AND BEYOND

As we venture further into the 21st century, the legacy of Enki in modern culture continues to evolve, reflecting the dynamic interplay between ancient mythology and contemporary values. The enduring fascination with Enki across various mediums—from academic research and digital media to environmental activism and spiritual exploration—highlights the deity's versatility and the universal appeal of his narratives. This ongoing engagement with Enki not only enriches our understanding of ancient Mesopotamian culture but also offers insights into the enduring human questions about creation, knowledge, and our relationship with the divine and the natural world.

The potential for Enki's legacy to inspire future generations lies in the adaptability of his myths to address the concerns and aspirations of the contemporary moment. As we face global challenges that require wisdom, creativity, and a commitment to sustainability, Enki's mythology serves as a reservoir of inspiration, offering ancient solutions to modern problems. The continued exploration and reinterpretation of Enki's stories promise to keep his legacy alive, fostering a dialogue between the past and the present that enriches our collective cultural heritage and guides us toward a more enlightened and balanced engagement with the world.

In conclusion, the future of Enki studies and his influence on modern culture is a testament to the power of ancient mythology to transcend time and cultural boundaries. As we continue to uncover, reinterpret, and integrate Enki's wisdom into our contemporary lives, his legacy serves as a beacon for those seeking to navigate the complexities of existence with insight, compassion, and balance. Through the ongoing exploration of Enki's mythology, we reaffirm the value of ancient narratives in addressing the perennial challenges of the human condition, ensuring that the wisdom of the past continues to illuminate the path forward in the 21st century and beyond.

# CONCLUSION

## SUMMARIZING ENKI'S WORLD ORDER

Enki's World Order, a concept deeply embedded in Mesopotamian mythology, encapsulates the deity's pivotal role in establishing the cosmos's laws, allocating resources, and ensuring the earth's fertility and well-being. This world order is not a static hierarchy but a dynamic balance of forces, reflecting Enki's wisdom in navigating the complexities of creation and governance. Through myths and legends, Enki is portrayed as a mediator and innovator whose interventions prevent chaos and promote harmony among gods and humans alike. His ability to solve problems with creativity and foresight, whether through the engineering of the Euphrates and Tigris rivers or the crafting of humanity from clay, showcases his integral role in sustaining life and civilization.

CONCLUSION

## THE ENDURING LEGACY OF ENKI

The legacy of Enki extends far beyond the ancient Sumerian texts and temples; it permeates various aspects of modern culture, from literature and art to environmentalism and digital media. Enki's attributes of wisdom, inventiveness, and compassion continue to resonate, offering insights into the human condition and our relationship with the natural world. This enduring appeal underscores the timeless nature of Enki's myths, serving as a source of inspiration and reflection for contemporary society. The fascination with Enki across different cultures and eras highlights the universal themes embedded in his stories, such as the quest for knowledge, the balance between order and chaos, and the stewardship of the earth's resources.

## CONTRIBUTIONS TO MESOPOTAMIAN SOCIETY

Enki's contributions to Mesopotamian society were profound, shaping its religious, social, and technological landscapes. As the god of water, wisdom, and creation, Enki was central to the Sumerians' understanding of the world and their place within it. His influence is evident in the development of agriculture, the establishment of laws, and the origins of writing, which collectively laid the foundations for one of the world's earliest civilizations. Enki's worship, characterized by rituals, festivals, and the construction of grand temples, not only reinforced social cohesion but also fostered a sense of identity and purpose among the Mesopotamian people. Through these contributions, Enki left an indelible mark on Mesopotamian culture, demonstrating the profound impact of deities on the development of human societies.

# CONCLUSION

## ENKI IN THE TAPESTRY OF WORLD MYTHOLOGIES

Enki's place in the tapestry of world mythologies is both unique and interconnected with the stories of deities from other cultures. Comparative mythology reveals shared motifs and themes, such as the trickster figure, the creator god, and the water deity, which resonate with Enki's characteristics and actions. This cross-cultural analysis not only enriches our understanding of Enki but also highlights the joint human endeavor to make sense of the cosmos, articulate moral and ethical values, and understand our place within the natural order. Enki's narratives, when viewed alongside those of gods from Greek, Egyptian, Hindu, and other traditions, contribute to a broader conversation about the nature of divinity, the challenges of creation, and the quest for balance and harmony in the universe.

## THE EVOLUTION OF ENKI'S WORSHIP

The evolution of Enki's worship, from ancient Sumerian rituals to contemporary spiritual practices, reflects the changing nature of human religiosity and the enduring relevance of ancient deities. Over millennia, Enki's image has been adapted and reinterpreted to meet different societies' spiritual needs, demonstrating mythological figures' flexibility and resilience. Today, Enki's legacy continues to inspire new forms of worship and spiritual exploration, blending ancient wisdom with modern perspectives on the divine. This ongoing evolution underscores the dynamic relationship between humanity and the gods, where ancient myths are continually reimagined to address contemporary questions and aspirations.

CONCLUSION

## REFLECTIONS ON THE NATURE OF DIVINITY

The study of Enki and other deities inspires reflections on the nature of divinity, which lead to a deeper consideration of the divine's function in both human life and the cosmos. Enki's narratives challenge us to consider the qualities that define divinity, such as wisdom, creativity, justice, and compassion, and their expression through the interactions between gods and humans. These reflections encourage a broader understanding of the divine as both immanent and transcendent, intimately involved in the world's workings yet beyond human comprehension. Through the lens of Enki's mythology, we are prompted to explore the complexities of faith, the mysteries of creation, and the possibilities for divine-human collaboration in shaping a just and harmonious world.

## BRIDGING MILLENNIA: ENKI'S ENDURING WISDOM

In the tapestry of ancient narratives and deities, Enki emerges not merely as a mythological figure confined to the clay tablets of Mesopotamia but as a beacon of wisdom, creativity, and balance that transcends time. Through the pages of this book, readers have journeyed into the heart of ancient civilization to uncover the layers of Enki's influence —from the life-giving waters of the Abzu to the profound depths of human knowledge and civilization's cradle. This exploration has revealed Enki as a multifaceted deity whose contributions to Mesopotamian society were foundational, not only in the tangible sense of agriculture and urban development but also in the intangible realms of ethics, governance, and the pursuit of harmony within the cosmos.

## CONCLUSION

What becomes clear through this journey is the timeless relevance of Enki's myths and teachings. In our modern era, where chaos and uncertainty often seem to prevail, Enki's narrative offers a reservoir of insight into navigating complexity with foresight and wisdom. His embodiment of dualities—order and chaos, creation and destruction—serves as a reminder of the balance necessary in our lives and societies. This book has not only illuminated the past but also cast a light on present challenges, encouraging you to draw upon ancient wisdom in addressing contemporary dilemmas. Enki's legacy, as explored in these pages, underscores the enduring power of myth to inspire, guide, and provide solace across ages.

Closing this chapter on Enki and the World Order, it is my hope that you are left with a sense of connection to a world far removed in time yet intimately linked through the shared human endeavor to understand our place in the universe. And that the investment in this exploration is rewarded with a deeper appreciation for the richness of human heritage and the complex tapestry of beliefs that have shaped our collective journey. Enki's story, resplendent with lessons of innovation, resilience, and the quest for equilibrium, resonates as a testament to the indomitable spirit of inquiry that defines us. Turning the final page reminds us that the wisdom of the ancients, which Enki embodies, continues to serve as a guiding light, encouraging us to face the future with hope, balance, and an ever-curious heart.

# GLOSSARY

**Abzu**: Primordial watery abyss ruled by Enki.

**Akkadian**: Semitic people; language of ancient Mesopotamia.

**Anu**: The sky god and father of Enki.

**Anunnaki**: Deities in Mesopotamian mythology, often associated with Enki.

**Archaeology**: Study of human history through excavation.

**Artifact**: Object made by humans, typically of cultural or historical interest.

**Cuneiform**: Ancient writing system used in Mesopotamia.

**Cosmology**: Study of the universe's origin and structure.

**Creation Myth**: Story explaining the universe's origins.

**Cultural Heritage**: Legacy of physical artifacts and intangible attributes inherited from past generations.

# GLOSSARY

**Deity**: A god or goddess.

**Divination**: Practice of seeking knowledge of the future.

**E-Abzu**: Enki's temple in Eridu.

**Ea**: Akkadian name for Enki.

**Ecology**: Branch of biology concerning interactions among organisms and their environment.

**Ecosystem**: Biological community interacting with its environment.

**Edin**: Sumerian term possibly related to the biblical Eden.

**Enki**: God of water, wisdom, and creation.

**Enlil**: The air god and brother of Enki.

**Eridu**: Ancient city believed to be Enki's domain.

**Esoteric**: Intended for or understood by a small number of people.

**Fertility**: Capability of producing life.

**Gilgamesh**: Hero of an epic Mesopotamian poem.

**Hieroglyphics**: Writing system using symbolic pictures.

**Inanna**: The goddess of love and war and sister of Enki.

**Irrigation**: Supplying land with water through channels.

**Lamentation**: Expression of deep sorrow or grief.

**Lexicon**: The vocabulary of a person, language, or branch of knowledge.

**Mesopotamia**: Region within the Tigris-Euphrates river system.

# GLOSSARY

**Mythology**: Collection of myths, especially one belonging to a particular religious or cultural tradition.

**Nammu**: The goddess of the ancient sea and mother of Enki.

**Nomadic**: People with no fixed residence, who move from place to place.

**Omen**: Event regarded as a portent of good or evil.

**Oral Tradition**: Knowledge, art, ideas, and cultural material conveyed verbally from one generation to another.

**Pantheon**: All the gods of a particular culture.

**Polytheism**: Belief in or worship of more than one god.

**Priesthood**: The office or position of a priest.

**Primordial**: Existing at or from the beginning of time.

**Ritual**: A religious or solemn ceremony consisting of a series of actions performed according to a prescribed order.

**Scribe**: A person who copies out documents, especially one employed to do this before printing was invented.

**Sumerian**: Relating to Sumer, an ancient region of southern Mesopotamia.

**Symbolism**: The use of symbols to represent ideas or qualities.

**Syncretism**: The amalgamation of different religions, cultures, or schools of thought.

**Tablet**: A flat piece of stone, clay, or wood, used as a writing surface.

**Theogony**: The genealogy of a group or system of gods.

GLOSSARY

**Tigris**: One of the two major rivers of Mesopotamia.

**Totem**: A natural object or animal believed by a particular society to have spiritual significance.

**Underworld**: The world of the dead in various religious traditions.

**Uruk**: Ancient Mesopotamian city, one of the world's first major cities.

**Water**: Element central to Enki's domain, symbolizing life and wisdom.

**Wisdom Literature**: Texts offering insights into ethics and philosophy.

**World Order**: Concept of a harmonious universe maintained by Enki.

**Ziggurat**: Massive structure built in ancient Mesopotamia.

**Zodiac**: Astrological system dividing the sky into twelve parts.

# SUGGESTED READINGS

- **Alster, Bendt** - *Proverbs of Ancient Sumer: The World's Earliest Proverb Collections*
- **Bertman, Stephen** - *Handbook to Life in Ancient Mesopotamia*
- **Black, Jeremy; Green, Anthony** - *Gods, Demons and Symbols of Ancient Mesopotamia: An Illustrated Dictionary*
- **Bottero, Jean** - *Religion in Ancient Mesopotamia*
- **Crawford, Harriet** - *Sumer and the Sumerians*
- **Dalley, Stephanie** - *Myths from Mesopotamia: Creation, the Flood, Gilgamesh, and Others*
- **Foster, Benjamin R.** - *Before the Muses: An Anthology of Akkadian Literature*
- **George, Andrew R.** - *The Babylonian Gilgamesh Epic: Introduction, Critical Edition and Cuneiform Texts*
- **Hallo, William W.; Simpson, William Kelly** - *The Ancient Near East: A History*
- **Jacobsen, Thorkild** - *The Treasures of Darkness: A History of Mesopotamian Religion*

## SUGGESTED READINGS

- **Kramer, Samuel Noah** - *Sumerian Mythology: A Study of Spiritual and Literary Achievement in the Third Millennium BC*
- **Kriwaczek, Paul** - *Babylon: Mesopotamia and the Birth of Civilization*
- **Leick, Gwendolyn** - *A Dictionary of Ancient Near Eastern Mythology*
- **Michalowski, Piotr** - *The Correspondence of the Kings of Ur: An Epistolary History of an Ancient Mesopotamian Kingdom*
- **Nemet-Nejat, Karen Rhea** - *Daily Life in Ancient Mesopotamia*
- **Oppenheim, A. Leo** - *Ancient Mesopotamia: Portrait of a Dead Civilization*
- **Postgate, J.N.** - *Early Mesopotamia: Society and Economy at the Dawn of History*
- **Roux, Georges** - *Ancient Iraq*
- **Van De Mieroop, Marc** - *A History of the Ancient Near East ca. 3000 - 323 BC*
- **Wolkstein, Diane; Kramer, Samuel Noah** - *Inanna, Queen of Heaven and Earth: Her Stories and Hymns from Sumer*